How to Adapt Anything into a Screenplay

How to Adapt Anything into a Screenplay

Richard Krevolin

WILEY

John Wiley & Sons, Inc.

Published by John Wiley & Sons, Inc., Hoboken, New Jersey
Published simultaneously in Canada

Design and production by Navta Associates, Inc.

For general information about our other products and services, please contact our Customer Care Department within the United States at (800) 762-2974, outside the United States at (317) 572-3993 or fax (317) 572-4002.

Wiley also publishes its books in a variety of electronic formats. Some content that appears in print may not be available in electronic books. For more information about Wiley products, visit our web site at www.wiley.com.

Library of Congress Cataloging-in-Publication Data:
Krevolin, Richard W., date.
  How to adapt anything into a screenplay / Richard Krevolin.
    p. cm.
  Includes bibliographical references.
  Filmography: p.
  ISBN 0-471-22545-2 (pbk. : alk. paper)
    1. Motion picture authorship. 2. Film adaptations. I. Title.
  PN1996 .K718 2003
  808.2'3—dc21

                                                                    2002027001

Printed in the United States of America

10 9 8 7 6 5 4 3 2 1

To Shana

To all my teachers, including John Furia, Joseph Bologna, Jeff Arch, and Coach Orgovan.

To my students, past, present, and future, for in the act of trying to teach you about the art and craft of writing, you have taught me more than you could ever know about being a better writer and human being. And for that, I am sincerely thankful.

And to all my readers, write boldly, without fear and with great passion.

Contents

Contents

Foreword

by Jeff Arch

When Rich Krevolin asked me to write the Foreword to his first book, *Screenwriting from the Soul,* I told him I'd be happy to do it. And I was—first of all because it was (and is) a mighty good and useful book, written by a USC cinema professor, no less, and second, because Rich said he'd take me to this really great Japanese noodle house in West L.A. that a lot of other people didn't know about yet, and that he would buy me a bowl of noodles there instead of paying me to write the Foreword. To further show you what a great guy Rich is, he also said I could pick whether I wanted udon noodles—the thick white ones that look like they could be somebody's insides—or soba noodles, which are thinner and brownish and resemble long athletic shoelaces. He also recommended iced tap water over the more expensive and lead-free bottled kind, and said I could keep my chopsticks.

You can see where I—where anyone—would jump at something like that.

So I wrote the Foreword and I did my best, and his book had really good sales anyway. Then, rather than leave well enough alone, Rich wrote *another* book, and asked me—superstition is the only reason I can figure—to think up a new Foreword for it.

Up until now I have written a bunch of screenplay adaptations—from two very serious nonfiction books, three novels, and a real howler (I hope) of a comedy to round things out. I have been hired and very nicely paid by studios or networks to write all of these scripts, except for the comedy, which I have developed on my own. What that means in real terms is that I have gone through two dozen boxes of #5 Rolling Ball Pilot Pens, five multipacks of highlighting markers in assorted colors, more than ten spiral notebooks where the spirals go along the top (I'm left-handed), three and a half computers, an uncountable number of floppy disks, at least two office chairs, a few household pets, and a generous amount of Advil. Plus I still have the same wife and children I started out with, and that ought to say something.

But here's the neat part, writingwise: In the cases where I have been in contact with the original authors of the books I've adapted, they have been elated that I was able to turn their work into a movie script and still have it be something they're proud of. If you want to know how rare that is, ask any authors you might know who've been through this.

So that's me, and now back to Rich. Let's review: He knows a great undiscovered noodle house in L.A., he's got a steady job teaching college students at a primo university, he's been on book tours, he's had his plays produced, his screenplays have been optioned and are on their way, and he got a really pretty girl to like him enough to marry him. So when someone like that writes a second book about screenwriting, it's time for all of us to sit up and pay attention. Especially since I get noodles out of this.

And I am not talking about just any noodles. These are Japanese noodles, which are totally healthy because they are served in Japanese restaurants, where almost *everything* is totally healthy—and if you don't believe me, then just consider this: There are like a ton of Japanese people living in Japan alone, and what do they have a lot of over there? Noodle houses. In fact there are more noodle houses per capita in Japan than there are monster puppets, and there are a lot of monster puppets over there, because that's where they made all those hilarious science fiction movies, where Tokyo is always getting creamed by enormous fearsome creatures who are furious that there is no place to park in that city. So they start tearing down all the buildings—while normal-sized people point and scream with bad dubbing and run panicking down the street, trying like hell to pretend that this is really happening. And what will every single one of these people tell you? That *it all starts with the script*.

Actually, they won't say that at all—and for that they probably *deserve* to be chased by monster fire-breathing puppets.

My point is this: Some of these movies were originals, and some were adaptations. Just like the movies we make over here. And whoever wrote them faced the same exact problems and asked the same exact questions that you and I, as screenwriters, face every single day. And it goes way beyond whether to pick udon or soba, all the way to the larger issues—issues that actually involve screenwriting, and for the purposes of this book, screenwriting that specifically deals with the transformation of a previously existing property—a book, a short story, a song, a magazine or newspaper story, even an earlier movie or television series—and probably some other things I'm not thinking of right now but I really need to finish this sentence—from its original form into the form of a modern professional screenplay that is guaranteed to take your agent way too long to read.

Some of you may be asking at this point, "Yes but how do I *get* an agent?" And while that is a totally valid question, it's not one I'm going to deal with here—because frankly, I just don't want to. Because even if you factor in the small handful of writers who were born with adequate representation, you'd still have to admit that the vast majority of us have to stumble into it on our own—which is exactly what you will do, when it's time. And even though you might be thinking that *today* would be a *really* good time, just in case it isn't, take heart—and let that part of your career unfold in its own uniquely maddening way. And besides, you won't even need an agent until you've written a couple of kickass screenplays—and if you feel you might need some help doing that, then you've come to the right place.

First of all, Rich really does teach this stuff—and not in the back room at some car wash, but like I said, at the University of Southern California, where a whole bunch of people went who are now multimillionaires and get top position in those "Hollywood's Power 100" lists more often than you and I get phone calls asking us if we're happy with our current long-distance service.

Do the names Lucas and Spielberg ring a bell? Zemeckis? Enough said. Because they went to USC, and now they have enough money to be signed up for any long-distance program they want— maybe up to three of them—without worrying about peak calling periods or anything. And they can even choose to pay other people to decide on calling plans for them, which is a highly elevated condition. Think about it.

Now I'm not saying that Rich taught these guys, because that would have been chronologically impossible. What I am saying is that if tomorrow's Lucas and Spielberg and Zemeckis are out there right now, then they are likely at one of a small handful of film schools in the world—one of which is USC—and if they're at USC, then they're probably going to take a course or two from Rich Krevolin, and all these things combined make it extremely possible that you and I will be standing in line to watch their movies one day.

And here he is, with a second book out now, that they will *definitely* be reading at USC—and if you want to see another whole generation of film school people riding around in limos and having agents before you do, then go ahead and put this book back on the shelf and move on and buy something else. Or go get a cinnamon-dark chocolate sprinkled latte with half foam and half Rice Krispies, or order an omelet made with only egg whites and *absolutely no carbs*, like everyone else does in the business, and then sit down with your friends and bitch about how your career isn't going anywhere.

(If the last part of that paragraph bothered you, then you're going to need a thicker skin. Hollywood is not the Boy Scouts. Hollywood is not even the Marines. Hollywood makes *movies* about the Marines—that's how tough Hollywood is. Picture a bunch of elite Special Ops guys, working you over while hackers empty out your bank account.)

Which brings me back to adaptations. Because while there are some things—a lot of things—that I know absolutely nothing about, there are a few other things I know at least a little about. And based on experience alone, along with some good old American dumb luck, I have happened to come into a little bit of knowledge in the area of screenplay adaptations over the years. They haven't all been *made*, and neither will yours or anyone else's. But whether you get that green light or not, it doesn't really change anything about the process itself—you still have to get from here to there, and you have to do it as best you can. So that when you deliver your draft, you'll know you've covered every base there is to cover.

Because the main thing is to keep growing as a writer. And the only way you're going to do that is to keep writing—and don't get caught letting someone else's definition of success define you. Success at writing means telling a good story with fluid command of the tools at hand while living a balanced life away from the keyboard. The rest, I promise, is all pretty much voodoo. Black magic. *Movie magic.*

And when it comes to the old originals versus adaptations debate, the truth is that neither one is easier, and that writing anything of lasting value is hard—really hard—and if you're doing your job right, then every single script you write will do its best to drive you absolutely out of your mind at some point. To come through all that, and emerge on the other side with a coherent and compelling story is one of the true pure joys in any writer's life. To be in the middle of it, though, is no darn fun sometimes—and like a pilot flying through a storm, even though you have your maps and your charts and radar, it still comes down to *you*—you alone, flying the thing—and your results will have a lot to do with how well you use the tools at hand.

So think of yourself as a pilot, and think of this fine book of Rich's, plus the other fine book he wrote, as just two of the maps and the charts and the radar you'll need for the times when those thunderclouds start coming at you and you want to get the best work out of yourself that you're capable of. Because I swear, when you do this thing right, it really does feel like flying. And you don't need an agent to feel that way, and you don't need anybody's permission, and you don't need an office on the lot and a great table everywhere and your name in the trades and a three-picture deal and a prewritten speech to the members of the Academy. I mean, all those things are *nice*, there's no doubt about it. But if you're a writer—really a writer—then you're going to be writing something anyway, always, because there's no earthly way that you can't.

In closing—yes, there is an end to this—I just want to say that I wish the best for each of you. I wish you fun and thrills and exalted moments, and aching dilemmas, and perfect act breaks, and many production bonuses, and all the other wonders of the screenwriter's life. And because it's the movies, I really do wish you, more than anything else, a happy ending. Lots of them. Because take it from a guy who's had one or two—there's nothing in the world like a happy ending.

Jeff Arch is the Oscar-nominated screenwriter best known for his original screenplay *Sleepless in Seattle,* which shot new life into the romantic comedy genre. Since then he has written original scripts, rewrites, and the following fiction and nonfiction book adaptations: *Exit the Rainmaker* for CBS, *The Georgia Waltz* for Ron Howard/Brian Grazer, *The Runaway* for Hallmark Hall of Fame, *Saving Milly* for CBS, *The Diary of V* for NBC, and *Dave Barry's Complete Guide to Guys,* an independent feature that Jeff will direct in 2003.

Preface

In almost every screenwriting seminar that I have ever taught, three related questions always seems to arise:

"Can you talk more about adaptations?"

"Where is the bathroom?"

"What are the rights issues, and in the end, what does the screenwriter owe the original text?"

This book will answer these and any other similar questions regarding the nature and craft of adaptations. Yes, I can and will talk about adaptations for hundreds of pages, so sit back and relax there, Kemosabe. And if you're still wondering, the bathroom is down the hall and on your left.

With that said, let me now reassure you that I will provide a nuts-and-bolts approach as well as an insider's view of Hollywood, complete with the angst, tragedy, and triumph of working and surviving within the Hollywood system. It is also worth noting that in any given year, a majority of films that are nominated for the Academy Award for Best Picture are adaptations. Just look at *Ordinary People, Terms of Endearment, Out of Africa, Driving Miss Daisy, The Silence of the Lambs, Schindler's List, Forrest Gump,* and *The English Patient.* In addition, many TV movies and miniseries are adaptations (*Dinotopia, The Diary of Anne Frank, The Mists of Avalon,* etc.). In the end, any way you look at it, adaptations are a significant part of the film and TV world and merit greater interest and attention.

After having adapted several of my own stage plays, a novel, and even a comic book for the screen, I've noticed a series of rules that have come into play each time I've approached the scary task of adaptation. Yes, there are specific unifying guidelines that can be implemented during the act and art of adaptation. This will be the first book to clearly articulate all these steps and present them in a systematic manner, outlining a proven five-step system to adapt anything for Hollywood, from a single-sentence story idea all the way to a thousand-page novel. Thus, I would argue that the method articulated in this book could also be used by any beginner trying to structure any story that he or she believes is screen- and scriptworthy, even if it is not an adaptation.

This system starts with breaking down the source material. Then it continues by outlining a series of stages that will lead you as you structure your story to fit the needs of a 120-page Hollywood screenplay. In fact, even if you aren't adapting a novel, but are merely adapting a story idea you've always had, this five-step process will be the perfect method to take you from concept to finished first draft.

I have used this five-step process with thousands of novelists, short story writers, playwrights, poets, journalists, and aspiring writers in seminars around the country and in my classrooms at the USC and UCLA film schools. Time and time again, I have seen how amazingly helpful it can be. In the same way that Syd Field's three-act paradigm or Chris Vogler's twelve-step mythic structure have saved writers tremendous amounts of time and heartache, I believe this five-stage process can serve as a series of guiding lights that will surely illuminate the dark and treacherous path of adaptation.

Acknowledgments

Even though only one name appears on the cover of this book, all books emerge out of the collaboration of many different voices, and a book on adaptations must by its very nature owe a great debt to many different people and works of art. Thus, I would like to take this opportunity now to personally thank the following individuals (in alphabetical order): Hal Ackerman, Jeff Arch, Dan Bern, Scott Bindley, Shane Black, Larry Brody, June "Super Agent" Rifkin Clark, Craig Clyde, Sharon Y. Cobb, Kathy Copas, Michael and Laura Cox, Michelle DeLong, Tom DeSanto, Bob Dylan, Amy Ellison, Fred Farley, Jessica Harris, Michael Hauge, Henry "Epic" Jones, Sherman and Evelyn Krevolin, Frederick Levy, Professor Odysseus Malodorus, Sandy and Chuck Masters, Linda McCann, Jim Noel, Bob "Coach" Orgovan, Simon Rose, Dale "Chip" Rosenbloom, Chip Rossetti, Kevin Ruane, Robin Russin, Jay "Legal Genius" Shanker, Dave Shuler, Travis and Carol Smith, Chris Vogler, Richard Walter, and Kathleen Annette "Katrina, Queen of Planetary Voices" Wilson.

A Short History of Adaptations

Whether I am reading a script written by a USC School of Cinema and Television student or by an aspiring screenwriter from somewhere in the country who has hired me as a consultant, I find one predominant misconception occurring over and over again in all the work I read—people think that screenwriting is easy and that since adaptations are derived from preexisting material, they are even easier.

Yes, most people believe that since they have been trained to write in English classes while they were in school, all they need to do is get a screenwriting format software program, find source material that is in the public domain, start typing, and bingo, when they hit page 120, pass them two metal brads, send the script out into the world, and WHAMMO! Just write them a check for a cool million.

But of course anyone who has ever struggled with the Hollywood machine and fought the good fight to get a script sold knows that this is far from true. Sure, there are the exceptional characters who land the big sale on their first script, but talk to most working screenwriters and they'll sing you the same tune: "Writing is hard. Good writing is even harder, and screenwriting may be the hardest of all. Usually it takes many drafts and ten or twenty finished scripts before a sale happens . . ."

First drafts are merely throat-clearing. The average writer usually goes through a series of drafts, no matter how experienced he or she may be. In fact, when I asked a veteran screenwriter how many scripts he wrote before he landed his first sale, he held his hand up to his neck and indicated a five-foot-tall stack. Yes, you must measure out work in feet, not in pages. It's a long process, comprised of years of hard work, a multitude of drafts, and huge Kinko's and postage bills.

So when someone does land a big fish and the cash register goes *ker-ching, ker-ching,* they deserve every penny they get paid. Sure, you can still hate them, but you can also be inspired by them and use your competitive jealousy to fuel yourself to finish your new baby and finally, instead of reading about others in *Daily Variety*, you can read about yourself!

Of course, there are no guarantees, and one cannot predict the next big fad in Hollywood. All you can do is write, rewrite, enter contests, go to seminars, send your work out there, get rejected, learn from rejection, and write some more. And lest you find this diatribe depressing, rest assured that those who do sell their scripts probably were ten-year overnight successes who got depressed and rejected regularly, and still get depressed and rejected regularly, but they do so in a cushy leather chair in their home office in their Beverly Hills mansion.

Okay, then, with that said and done, the essential issue is simply this: Ideas are a dime a dozen, good ideas are a dollar a dozen, and great ideas are even more rare, but no matter how stellar your premise is, there remains the all-important issue of execution. Sure, it's easy to talk about the idea you've always had for a movie, but it's a hell of a lot harder to pull it off. Just ask your taxicab driver who's pitching you his concept as he drives you to the airport or your waiter who's tossing his idea at you along with your Caesar salad. Everyone's a screenwriter these days, but a scarce few have the patience, passion, and persistence to do the series of drafts and put in the time to really work the story to the point where it must be before you should submit it, and someone will take you seriously.

Most of the movies that come out of Hollywood are mediocre, so it is only natural that many people believe that if they, too, write a mediocre script, soon they will be joining the esteemed ranks of the Writers Guild. Of course, such is not the case, and to break through, you must write an Academy Award–caliber script. (And then, if you like and are so inclined, you can produce mediocre work for the rest of your life.)

But wordsmith beware, the number-one mistake made by aspiring screenwriters is simply this: People hand in their scripts before they are ready. Remember, Hollywood is not a forgiving town, first impressions are lasting ones, and you only get one chance. So hold off. Make sure it's ready, and don't burn that bridge until after you've crossed it.

In the end, then, it is the quality of the script that means more than anything else, and that ephemeral sense of quality is developed only through hard work. No matter how good the original source material is for your adaptation, you must make it better, you must make it sing, and you must make it a work of art that stands on its own as a screenplay that was merely inspired by another work. And if you can fashion all your scenes with compelling highs and lows, your script will become a beautiful symphony and people will pay to hear it played over and over again.

With that said, it would be foolhardy to jump straight into an exploration of screen adaptations without first having a deep grounding in the origins and history of storytelling and adaptations. In Japan, master ceramicists have their apprentices spend two years merely kneading the clay and learning about the background of this art form. Screenwriting is really no different. You need to spend time noodling around in the art form, and to be clear as to where you are going, you should really be grounded in the history of where screenwriting came from. So, then, let us start with a short history lesson that might prove useful.

An Abridged History of Storytelling and Adaptation

FADE IN:

Int. Cave, Lascaux, France, 17,000 B.C.E.—Night

Storytelling is a part of us, programmed deep within our DNA. Look at the ancient cave paintings in Lascaux, France. They are not static portraits but moving images, the first movies, the first recorded signs of man's need to tell stories, to empower himself and perpetuate the race. His survival hinged upon it.

Simply put, if cave guy number one could convey to cave guy number two how he slayed the animal that was his primary source of nourishment, he could hoist his children up onto his shoulders instead of forcing them to stand on the ground and start from the same place he did decades earlier. Stories give us a proverbial leg up and represent the building blocks of society. And the art of adaptation is merely a transference of forms, a play of genres.

In the past, you told your story by painting a cave wall; today, you tell your version of the same story by writing it as a screenplay. The static cave wall painting is transformed into a digitally projected, THX, Dolby, Surround Sound, 35 mm cinematic movie.

CUT TO:

Ext. Middle Eastern Mountaintop Altar, 2100 B.C.E.—Day

In ancient times, when things weren't going so well, your average pagan priest attempted to appease the gods by a ritual sacrifice of a few virgins. For a while, this seemed to work. However, soon enough, populations started to dwindle and there were no virgins left, so there had to be a better way to solve society's worst problems.

Enter Abraham, the patriarch of the Jewish people. In fact, many Hebraic scholars argue that the pivotal moment in Western civilization occurs in the book of Genesis when at the very last moment, God sends an angel to instruct Abraham to sacrifice a ram instead of his son, Isaac. This is the first recorded instance of the use of a scapegoat, and the birth of the precedence of symbol over object. It is the moment of the ascendancy of the symbolic sacrifice over the murderous urge, when the power of image, of the symbol, of the myth, becomes primary and the aggressively violent death urge is put to rest along with other primitive human ways.

This is no less than the beginning of modern man, a man of language, of words, and of symbols that take the place of actions. A modern man who adapts to circumstances, taking one form of ritual storytelling and transforming it into another. The ram takes the place of the boy, the screenplay takes the place of the novel, the circle continues . . .

CUT TO:

Ext. The Tomb of Menna, Egypt, 1300 B.C.E.—Day

In ancient Egypt, the scribe Menna is buried in a tomb that features an elaborate story painting. The painting tells its tale by juxtaposing a series of images that can be read from the lower left-hand corner and working one's way up. One may even think of it as a detailed storyboard for a modern screenplay, telling of the process of harvesting wheat and the scribe's role in recording this yearly ritual. It also tells of taxes and the ramifications for being late paying those taxes. Like Trajan's column, which can be read if one wanders round and round the column, the story unfolds like a comic book, a work of sequential art that needs to be read in a specific order if the story is to make sense.

The story codification process begins to unfold. The oral tradition is being transformed by more permanent means. Stories once told over and over again are now adapted for posterity by being entombed and enshrined forever in stone.

CUT TO:

Ext. Greek Amphitheater, Athens, 400 B.C.E.—Day

Theater storytelling is about magic, transformation. There is a religious aspect to going to the theater or the movies. Good dramatic action serves a shamanistic, cathartic, priestlike purpose. The goal of any storyteller is to craft a tale so entertaining that we get wrapped up in the action and are taken to a feverish pitch, to a point of religious fervor. In ancient Greece, the theater was part of the culture's religious ceremonies, and all classes of citizens and noncitizens attended. The problems of the cultures were acted out onstage and in doing so, the theater became the scapegoat, the surrogate place where the culture could be cleansed.

Today, you go to the theater or the movie house to sit in a dark womb with a bunch of strangers and vicariously experience this human transformation. Like the Greeks, for whom theater was a communal and religious gathering wherein the fears and desires of the culture could be exorcised and expressed, modern-day stage plays and movies let us come together to create a new sense of community. When we sit together in the audience, we become part of a larger whole, one with the group, and gain a sense of fellowship, even if it is only for two hours.

Humans want to grow, and will gladly pay to see the transformation of other human beings. The ancient windswept Greek stage and the modern, air-conditioned multiplex theater serve the same societal purpose. By watching someone experience an epiphany and as a result undergo a transformation onscreen, as an audience member, you are not exempt; you, too, are transformed. Life-altering personal change, all in two hours for a mere nine dollars, while most therapists charge at least a hundred an hour. So millions of people go back to the movies every weekend, and the popular films, those that are embraced by the culture, succeed in perpetuating a new set of myths that can provide answers to the hard questions of being alive.

CUT TO:

Int. the Globe Theater, London, 1583—Night

Shakespeare's new Globe Theater is built south of the Thames. Theater is not considered a legitimate, moral aspect of society, so Shakespeare's theater is not allowed to be constructed north of the Thames, where the rest of God-fearing London society thrives. Instead, it is banished to the south bank of the Thames, where in this conservative British climate, all the whoremongers, prostitutes, moneylenders, pimps, and actors are forced to try to ply their trades.

Yet the power of stories cannot be ostracized from culture. Shakespeare's adaptations of ancient historical tales are so moving that the queen invites him to court and his plays become the toast of the town. Theater becomes civilized, accepted, and even celebrated. The ancient Greek stories played out on the amphitheater stages of

Athens were adapted, retooled, and retold by Shakespeare for his stage. Today, these same tales are constantly being reinvented once again in the form of such films as *Ten Things I Hate About You*, *O*, and *Shakespeare in Love*. Adaptations live on . . .

CUT TO:

Int. Warner Brothers Studio, 1927—Day

An adaptation of Alfred Cohn's story "The Day of Atonement" and Samson Raphaelson's hit Broadway play of the same name, *The Jazz Singer* is released and is a huge hit. Contrary to popular belief, *The Jazz Singer* is not the first film with sound or a synchronized sound and picture. It is, however, the first film to use synchronized sound for narrative purposes. In other words, now picture and sound are united for a single purpose—storytelling. And with this advance comes the need for the modern screenplay incorporating both images and dialogue.

FADE OUT:

FADE IN:

Int. Your House, the Global Village, Present Day—Dawn

Now, with the computer and digital revolutions, we are on the cusp of many new advances. How they will affect storytelling, screenplays, adaptations, and our whole notion of filmic art remains to be seen. So, you begin writing your own adaptation . . .

2

Professor K.'s Five-Step Adaptation Process

You've come across something that would make a great movie. Whether it's a series of letters in your attic, an article in your hometown newspaper, a story in an old book you picked up at a garage sale, or some scrawlings on the wall of the bathroom, you are convinced that this concept, this story you've discovered, will provide the perfect source material for a Hollywood blockbuster. You don't need a release or option, since the source material you've stumbled upon is public domain, or better yet, you've already gone out and done the work to secure the rights. (If not, please see chapter 3 on legal issues.)

Either way, you are now ready to go to script, but where the heck do you begin? How do you transform a 3-page article into a 110-page script? Or if you are adapting a 500-page classic Russian novel and transporting it to modern American soil, the question still begs to be answered: How do I compress 500 pages into a 120-page screenplay? Please, tell me, where the heck do I begin?

Don't fret, my friend. If you only remember one thing from reading this entire study on the art and craft of adaptations, make sure it is this: You really don't owe anything to the original source material. Yes, it might have been their story once, but the point is, it's your story now. The credits will read, Screenplay by YOU based upon a story by some lesser dead figure like Shakespeare. The key thing here is the three-letter word "YOU." No matter who the story used to belong to, it's now yours. You will be judged by how you choose to tell your tale, and no matter how good the original story was, it's your ass on the line now. You will get credit for making it sing with clarity and purpose, or for bastardizing and soiling it beyond repair.

After watching the wonderful adaptation of the first book of *The Lord of the Rings*, I visited the men's room on the way out of the theater. Since it was a three-hour-long film, as soon as the movie was over, almost the entire male population that saw *The Lord of the Rings* was in the john with me. And that was when I overheard a young man in the urinal stall next to me turn to his buddy and say, "Yo, dude, wasn't that awesome? It was totally like the novel."

I do think *The Lord of the Rings* was an awesome adaptation; however, I don't feel that way as a result of it being "totally like the novel." It was awesome because even though it shared many similarities to the novel, it seemed to truly capture the essence, the spirit, the soul of the novel. That, then, is what I believe the key to successful adaptation really is—not to do a verbatim and faithful transcription, which is in many ways impossible anyway, but to capture the truth of the original work and convey that onscreen.

In other words, the key point here to remember is that you are now free to create a new story inspired by the source material. Think of yourself as a Supreme Court justice searching for the spirit of the law, instead of abiding by the letter of the law. You can combine characters; eliminate whole sections; add scenes; change times, dates, places; do whatever needs to be done to make the script work. That, then, is Rule Number 1:

You owe nothing to the original text!

You needed the original text to get started and to inspire you, but now that you are moving into the world of scripts and Hollywood storytelling, new rules apply. And the only real bottom line is Rule Number 2:

If it makes for a good story, it stays.
If not, it must be trashed!

Yes, I know there might be a scene, detail, or character that you don't want to part with, but if it isn't completely necessary to push the story forward, it must go. The only rules that apply here are the rules of Hollywood storytelling. And Hollywood storytelling is based on this simple premise:

An engaging character overcomes tremendous obstacles to reach a desirable goal.

That is it. Beauty of language, scintillating cerebral concepts, and political or social issues are all well and good, but nine times out of ten, they are mere window dressing. They do not help your writing; in fact, many times they get in the way of the story and should be expunged. A screenplay is not a literary form, it is a mere blueprint for a film. Thus, screenwriting should not concern itself with preaching ideologies or utilizing gorgeous prose. This is not to say that there is no room for big ideas and good writing. Of course there is. What I am saying is simply that most aspiring screenwriters need to stay focused on the story first and foremost. No matter how important your ideas are or how beautiful your prose is, if the story is not compelling, you are in trouble. Big trouble.

In screenwriting, all fat must be sheared away. Screenwriting is a highly disciplined form of storytelling, one that comes closer to poetry writing than to many forms of prose. Screenwriting is, in fact, probably the best discipline to teach you the rules and structure of storytelling and is thus inherently valuable to any writer. Whether your script sells or not, I can guarantee you that you will learn a tremendous amount about your story in the process of restructuring it to fit the screen. Every time I have taken one of my stage plays and transformed it into a screenplay, I have inevitably gone back afterward and rewritten the stage play as a result of seeing the essential story elements that were missing in the original. These story moments only came into being and to my attention as a result of the rigorous restructuring that I had to engage in to make my story work as a screenplay.

Take the Nestea plunge of screenwriting. Remember, as a screenwriter, you are not constrained and limited, you are free to create and explore. And yes, of course, if you are doing a historical piece about the assassination of Abe Lincoln, you can't have Honest

Abe live through that fateful night he was shot by John Wilkes Booth. No matter how liberating the act of adaptation should be, in the case of historical and biographical efforts about known people and events, you do have the onus to maintain a certain degree of accuracy.

Yet there is even a good deal of leeway here, too, for no one knows exactly what was said or felt by the major players during, before, and after these grand historical events. Your job is to understand these situations based upon your research and the historical facts that exist and then fabricate your version. And if you do it well, no one can prove that the main players in the story didn't utter those very words and that things, in fact, didn't occur according to your version.

The main point here is simply this: In the context of an adaptation, you are free and in fact you have the burden to make the story better. It must be clearer, move faster, and be funnier than the source material. It must be more action-packed, thrilling, and sexy than the original. Good adaptations can never include all elements of the source material, so the art of adaptation becomes one of distillation, and I'm not talking sour mash whiskey here. The gifted adaptor knows his or her limitations and can find the theme, the crux, the heart and soul of the piece he or she is confronted with. That is their task and their burden. Even though elements are left out, the audience should feel as if the story itself remains intact. In the best-case scenarios, this will, in fact, lead the story to be improved.

If you embrace this task and burden, you are well on your way to writing an award-winning adaptation. But now you may ask, exactly where do I begin? If I am to take baby steps, do I start with the right foot or the left, my toes or my heel?

The answer is simply this: All you need to start is an idea, and that idea need only be encapsulated in a single word. Inevitably I hear the groans and the gasps of "Excuse me?"

Yes, friends, it is that simple. One teeny-weeny word. To begin, you need to be able to write one single word.

Yes, you can do it. I know you can. So, then, it all begins with . . .

Step 1: The Word

That is all. Find a single word that encapsulates the theme of your work. In the end, movies all come down to a single concept, a single word. The novel you are adapting might deal with myriad and sundry themes and events, but the script you are writing from this multilayered novel must be reinvestigated and reduced to a single word. Pick a good movie and you'll see that it is about one thing. *Titanic* was about love. In fact, many movies are about love. However, please don't get bogged down by this single word. Instead, use it as a starting point as you move forward. In addition, this word can also be used as a scouring pad to knock out those elements that don't correspond and to keep you focused.

Step 2: The One–Two Punch Logline

Can you write two full and complete sentences? Then you are ready to move on to step 2. Yet beware, because writing two sentences that succinctly encapsulate the gist of your story (not the theme) is a far trickier task than it seems. But this is a valuable discipline. It will allow you to clearly see what your movie is, which will make the writing easier, and down the line, it will help you in marketing your film.

If this is starting to seem a bit overwhelming, don't fret. I'll slow down. These two sentences need to follow this pattern:

The One Punch—Genre and Films

The "one punch," the first sentence of your description, should begin with the genre and then follow with preexisting films within the genre that when combined as examples give a good sense of your story. Since Hollywood is a place driven by fear, there is a desire to make films that are "similar to but also different from" successful preexisting films. Thus, you want, you need to cite other successful films as a precedent for the success of your film.

13

With this in mind, *Shanghai Noon* would be described as "an action-comedy movie in the vein of *Enter the Dragon* meets *High Noon*." Genre is significant because it dictates tone and feel for the film. Then the preexisting films you mention within that genre further clarify the exact nature of the tone. There is a big difference between a romantic comedy in the vein of *There's Something About Mary* and one in the vein of *Sleepless in Seattle*. Both are definitely romantic comedies, but they would occupy very different places on the romantic comedy spectrum.

Besides using genres and preexisting films to help define the story you are telling, they also help define the story in very few words. For example, you can define *Star Wars* in four words by saying that it is *High Noon* in space, or *Roxanne* as a modern-day American *Cyrano*. However, be careful of relying too much on known films or stories in your logline, because they can limit your ability to clearly see the true identity of your own piece. This then takes us to the second sentence of your two sentences.

The Two Punch—Plot

Not theme, plot. If you claim your script tells the tale of good triumphing over evil, you are merely espousing a vague thematic gesture that applies to many tales. In essence, your theme has already been articulated in your single word. We're moving on to bigger and better things here. Plot. Story. Don't tell me about this being the story of corruption, tell me this is a tale of a single mom who, even though she is merely a paralegal, helps win the largest lawsuit in American history. If you do this well, you will have mastered the art of the plot-based logline. The logline is the plot articulated in as few words as possible. It is the single sentence you see in *TV Guide* that describes the movie you are about to watch. And once you master your logline, you are well on your way to merrily rolling along to receiving an Academy Award nomination for best screenplay, and your star, Julia Roberts (*Erin Brockovich*), might just get an Oscar, too.

My favorite single sentence comes from the movie poster for the James Cameron film *True Lies*. It reads, "Before he said I do, she should have found out what he did." In a few words, we are intrigued and hooked by the story concept. Look at movie posters and start to read the promotional tags that are featured next to the images. How do the marketers entice you with as few words as possible? Your job is to mimic these loglines in your own development of your material.

If you are having trouble with your single-sentence story pitch, try the "what if" exercise. Many times a story begins with the two words "WHAT IF?" and to really nail your story, you might also need to throw in the two words "AND THEN?" For example, what if an asteroid the size of Texas was hurtling toward Earth? Okay, good basic premise, but nothing without the "AND THEN": The world's greatest oil drilling team, led by Bruce Willis, has 72 hours to stop it. Don't give away the ending, just set up the story parameters.

And please, don't devalue the power of this second, plot-driven sentence. Loglines sell scripts. When you are finished with your script, many of you are going to be interested in marketing it. And the key to marketing it will be your ability to convey the story in a single sentence. If that sentence is compelling enough, agents, managers, and lawyers will want to read it and, if they like it enough, sign you. Then they will also rely upon that very same single sentence to entice their buyers to read it. So, like it or not, your script sinks or swims based upon your logline.

Yes, movie buffs, Hollywood is logline driven. But rest easy there, chief. If you need help with loglines, read *TV Guide*. See how even the greatest filmic masterpieces of Western culture are crystallized into single sentences. *American Beauty* is reduced to "A middle-aged man starts working out to impress his daughter's pretty friend." *Citizen Kane* becomes "The tale of the rise and fall of newspaper tycoon Charles Foster Kane." Yes, it's reductive, but it's also necessary. Don't fight it. The discipline of defining your story will only help you clarify it. And trust me if the single-sentence story concept doesn't excite people, what makes you believe 120 pages of it will?

Okay, now you've nailed the genre, cited similar preexisting films, and clarified the story concept. Your logline excites you and everyone you tell it to. Congratulations. This is no easy feat and can take weeks in and of itself. Once you've finally done it, you are ready to move to . . .

Step 3: The Big Seven

There are now seven essential questions that must be answered before you move forward. The answers to these questions will be essential in helping you clarify and define your story. Please rest assured, it's not worth freaking out about the answers to these questions. They are merely starting points to help you further define your story. In many cases, the answers to these questions will change over the course of writing your script, but these seven questions have proven themselves to me over and over again as the single best place to start and a great place to visit while developing the story. God bless, write hard and don't quit.

The Big Seven

1. Who is your main character? (You can only have one.)
2. What does your main character want/need/desire? (In other words, what is his or her dramatic problem? Bear in mind that this dramatic problem needs to be articulated in terms of both an inner and an outer need.)
3. Who/what keeps him from achieving what he wants? (Who/what are the apparent and true antagonists?)
4. How in the end does s/he achieve what s/he wants in an unexpected, interesting, and unusual way?
5. What are you trying to say by ending the story this way? (What is your theme, and do you have any unifying filmic devices?)
6. How do you want to tell your story? (Who should tell it, if anyone, and what narrative devices should you employ?)
7. How do your main character and any supporting characters change over the course of the story?

Now, before you go off all half-cocked about your answers to these seven questions, let's look at them a little more closely.

1. *Who is your main character?* (You can only have one.)

   Novels can be filled with characters, but although films may be populated with large ensembles, in the end, Hollywood story-telling is primarily driven by a single protagonist. Thus, you really need to decide who your main character is. Not your five main characters, but your *one* main character. Start and end the movie with this person and follow him or her throughout the script. They are the heart and soul of your story and if they aren't likable, you are dead. So make sure they have a rich inner life and lots of fascinating character traits.

2. *What does your main character want/need/desire?* (In other words, what is his or her dramatic problem? Bear in mind that this dramatic problem needs to be articulated in terms of both an inner and an outer need.)

   If your movie is only as good as your main character, it is equally true that your main character is only as interesting as their dramatic problem. So make sure that what they want/need/desire is something that all of us in the audience also want/need/desire. The top three answers to this question are usually love, money, and life (i.e., survival). Be careful of vague answers here. Love is a valid desire, but usually it comes as a reward for getting the pot of gold or killing the bad guy. Film as a concrete, visual medium demands that the want/need/desire be filmable. In other words, love is great, but how do you film it? Sex, a kiss, or a pot of gold are much easier to see on film.

   Therefore, most films usually present wants/needs/desires that are tangible things that one can bring to sell at the pawn-shop or can be physically embodied in the form of a person or large object. Harry Potter wants the quidditch trophy and to overcome Lord Voldemort. This is the exterior want, which should also be mimicked in the form of an inner want/need/emotional desire such as respect or popularity or love. And so Harry's desires for success on the quidditch field and against Lord Voldemort represent a deeper need for family, community, and love. The goal, then, is to have these inner and outer wants correspond and work together to drive the character.

Also, these wants/needs/desires can change over the course of the story, but remember, wants/needs/desires are the main factor that engages audiences, so they must be clearly articulated early. At first, Dorothy in *The Wizard of Oz* wants to run away from home; then, after landing in Oz, she wants to go back home. As these goals change over the course of the story, the audience must understand what the NEW wants/needs/desires are at all times.

3. *Who/what keeps him from achieving what he wants?* (Who/what are the apparent and true antagonists?)

Your movie is only as good as your bad guy and the tremendous obstacles that rise along the path of your main character's journey. So, it is not your job to be nice and make your protagonist's life easy, but instead to fill his life with hardships, conflicts, and obstacles. In addition, your antagonist can change over the course of the story, and the apparent antagonist may become an ally while an apparent ally may become the true antagonist. Finally, Mother Nature may also become one of the antagonists, or even the true antagonist, as in *The Perfect Storm*.

4. *How in the end does s/he achieve what s/he wants in an unexpected, interesting, and unusual way?*

We know that James Bond will save the world again at the end of the movie, but we are not sure how. The key to filmic storytelling then becomes not about the WHAT of your story, but about the HOW. The events that happen in your story must always be fresh and unexpected. The audience thinks they want to anticipate what is going to happen, but in reality, they want to be tricked. They want to say to themselves, "Oh, now I see." The end of *The Sixth Sense* works because we thought we knew what was happening, but once we discover the truth, we hit ourselves on the forehead and say, "That's cool and it makes sense. I'm such an idiot. I should've figured that out."

We are pleasantly surprised. We see the truth of what was really happening in the story. The ending becomes legitimate and clear even though we weren't capable of seeing it that way when we were first watching it. If this is done properly, the audience is moved; if it is not done legitimately, the audience becomes angry and rejects the story. It is your job to plant story elements throughout the script so that even though the ending is unexpected, interesting, and unusual, the audience will see in retrospect, that it is also inevitable.

5. *What are you trying to say by ending the story this way?* (What is your theme, and do you have any unifying filmic devices?)

Movies are driven by themes, and usually there are also several unifying filmic devices (UFDs) that can be thought of as recurring visual, narrative, or dialogical motifs. The recurrence of certain elements is a dead giveaway for the conscious and unconscious themes of the author and/or *auteur*. It is very valuable to look at what constantly reappears in your work (character types, episodes, events, lines of dialogue, props, etc.). These recurring events, people, and lines of dialogue reveal a deeper inner meaning if they are analyzed from an objective distance. If a writer desires to add greater power and complexity to his or her work by incorporating certain thematic elements, he or she can consciously intersperse various UFDs throughout the work. In other words, specific elements of a story, like the color red as well as red roses in *American Beauty*, are more than just props. They are UFDs that are reincorporated back into the movie later, adding resonance to the film as a whole.

In the end, your theme is determined by the way you end your story. Climax and conclusion dictate the overriding thematic statement of your story. Therefore, be conscious of how you end your story and what you are saying by utilizing such an ending.

6. *How do you want to tell your story?* (Who should tell it, if anyone, and what narrative devices should you employ?)

This is the most undervalued and most highly significant question of all. Of course you want to tell your story well, but the key thing here is exactly how you want to manipulate the scene order and what devices you will employ along the way. Do you start in the middle and work backward? Do you use voice-over or flashbacks? Do you have a narrator and if so, what role will he or she play in the film? In fact, your narrator might not necessarily even be your main character. Many times, when you are on a third or fourth draft of a story that just doesn't seem to be working, the answer is not in the story itself but in the style/structure of the storytelling. So, pay heed to this question and answer it carefully.

7. *How do your main character and any supporting characters change over the course of the story?*

This, then, is the question that embodies the golden rule of change. How does the main character change over the course of the script? Is this change justified and satisfying? Does the audience believe the change? Even though the story may only take place in the course of one night, does the change happen in legitimate, gradual stages so that by the end it seems justified and valid? If there is no change, your audience will feel robbed. So your film must have a character who arcs and changes if you want your audience to experience this arc along with the character and thus grow or change a little bit by being exposed to your story.

Step 4: The Scene-O-Gram

The scene-o-gram is a good starting point for you to see the major beats of your story. It allows the writer to chart out the entire course of his story on one page and see what he or she may really have.

Obviously, you will expand and inevitably alter much of the scene-o-gram over the course of further developing your story.

This scene-o-gram is a variation on an original concept developed by a colleague, a wonderful screenwriting instructor at UCLA named Hal Ackerman. Fill in as much as you can, even things that will never appear in your movie, like the titles for each act. The more you can add to the scene-o-gram, the better sense you will get of the major beats and sequences in your script.

However, before you rush off and fill in all those blank boxes, let me elaborate upon the basic tenets of the three-act Hollywood structure, so that you have a better sense of where to put your scenes. There are no clear act demarcations in a film; however, a trained eye will soon come to see that there really is something to this act break thing. Act divisions are not as invisible and difficult to discern as you might think. The more you practice analyzing a film, the easier it will be for you to see them.

To further ease your understanding of act structure, let me explain a sense of the goals of each act.

Act I Goals

1. Have a compelling premise. I don't care how well you write, if you are trying to break through into Hollywood with your screenplay, you need to write a movie with a compelling premise. Scripts are not sold on writing quality; they are sold on ideas, concepts, and premises. Hence, yours better be something that makes other people say, "Wow, that would make an amazing film!" Like it or not, the people who are going to try to sell your film are going to use a single sentence to do so. Thus you have to make sure that sentence is compelling, vibrant, and fresh!

2. Make sure the reader can identify with your main character and many of the supporting characters. Most people don't identify with the rich, the mean, or the stupid. So, in general, main characters tend to be well-meaning members of the

working class trying to better themselves. Yes, Julia Roberts once played a movie star in *Notting Hill* (albeit an unloved misunderstood, innocent movie star). But think of all her other roles—a single mother/paralegal *(Erin Brockovich)*, a streetwalker *(Pretty Woman)*, a hairstylist *(Runaway Bride)*, and so on. If your protagonist must be a zillionaire, a gangster, a cheat, or some type of inherently unsympathetic person, make sure he has lots of redeeming qualities: kindness, amiability, gentleness, humor, compassion, or eccentricity.

The only other way to go is to have your rich, mean, unsympathetic protagonist become an underdog very quickly by being stripped of his rank, and then instantly he's become one of us and entirely more engaging. In the end, Hollywood storytelling is a great democratic art. It must appeal to millions of people—and let's be honest, most of them don't like their jobs, their bodies, their income levels, or any number of other things about their lives. Hence the predominance of the escapist fantasy of Hollywood tales that feature regular Joes and Janes who break through the system and win. You are the dream weaver—always keep that in mind, please.

3. Don't introduce too many new characters too quickly. Most of the scripts I read represent bewildering experiences that require long hours of flipping of pages back and forth. This is a direct result of the screenwriter introducing way too many characters in the first several pages. The human mind can only process so much. You as the author may be familiar with all the people who populate your story, but the reader is not. Relax there, Speedy, and slowly introduce the main character and then have others introduced through his eyes, his experiences. The rest of the characters are supporting cast members. Start with the main character, follow him, and end with him. As you need to, have him meet the rest of the players and we will slowly assimilate all the people we need to know.

4. There must be a great deal at stake. In other words, is there enough sense of magnitude? This may be the most common problem in screenwriting. What is at stake? I am always

screaming at my students, "WHO CARES? RAISE THE STAKES!" There must be clarity as to what is at stake and what will happen if the main character fails to achieve his or her goals. If not, I, as a member of the audience, will not care deeply about the outcome.

5. Hook your audience with the dramatic problem of your story.
6. Include an inciting incident.
7. Clarify the main character's goals, that which is at stake as a result of this goal, and the necessity for the character to achieve his or her goals.
8. Have a galvanizing moment that twists the story in a new direction, forever changing the life of the main character and launching us into Act II.
9. The genre must be clear. There is no room for a historical romantic comedic teen movie. Know what genre your picture is and abide by the rules of that genre. In a comedy, you can't have people dying all over the place, unless of course it is a black comedy in which the comedy comes out of FUNNY deaths. The key thing here is that as the author you must know exactly how far you can go within your genre. The tone must be nailed and must be consistently followed throughout the story.

Act II Goals

1. Build your story. Take the stakes established in Act I and raise them even higher. You think it can't get any harder for our hero, but alas, 'tis possible. In addition, the conflicts grow more and more intense.
2. Reverse expectations. In doing so, you should force your protagonist to take greater risks.
3. Provide more and more interesting obstacles to prevent him or her from achieving his or her goals.
4. Don't be boring. Don't be too talky. Keep a sense of urgency and danger. Yes, the second act is where you can deepen your

characters and have revelatory monologues in which they reveal the unplumbed depths of their gorgeous souls, but still, you gotta keep moving forward. Always onward and upward, with no fluff, no fat, only lean, muscular prose.

5. The dramatic problem must now represent something larger than the protagonist's life. If your protagonist fails, so what? SO WHAT? I gotta really care by now. Even though I've had three Starbuck's cappuccinos and my bladder is on the verge of bursting, I'm afraid to go to the bathroom because I fear I'll miss something crucial. Keep their swollen bladders glued to the seats and you've won.

6. Keep a constant sense of danger, threat, and tension, especially in the second act. In many scripts I read, there seems to be an awful lot of people sitting around gabbing, and the story never seems to be going anywhere. From the get-go, the story needs to build. Then, as it builds, the tension constantly needs to increase and a sense of threat needs to remain present. On what page does your inciting incident occur? The later it does, the more trouble you're going to be in.

Something important, or as William Goldman calls it, "A whammo!," needs to happen every ten pages. Every ten pages, something needs to reignite the flame under the reader's ass. In some cases, someone dying isn't enough. Unless we see him die and his death changes the nature of the conflict in the story, you still haven't gone far enough. Have you seen *Behind Enemy Lines?* In this film, we keep thinking things can't get worse for the Owen Wilson character, but of course, they do. And as the story moves forward, we realize that it is just not one man's life that is at stake, but that in fact he is involved in a situation that could conceivably ignite World War III.

7. Your dialogue must not be overwritten. People rarely say what they're really thinking. When they do, it's filtered, candy coated, homogenized, and pared down to elicit a desired response. More aptly put, people say the things they say to get what they want, especially in film. All the genuine moments

involving the dialogue in your story have one thing in common: they're short. The logic here is simple. The less time it takes to make your point, the more clear it will be. It forces the reader to notice. A slow rain inconveniences people, but a flash flood gets their attention. Keeping that in mind, remember that the dialogue can't be too on the nose. Dialogue is a subtle business; be a little softer on the keys.

One more quickie on dialogue. Don't ever ask yourself, "Would a person actually say this?" Ask yourself, "Given everything we know about this character, the world he lives in, and the events that have occurred thus far, would he say this?" People don't go to the movies to hear the same conversations they hear every day, they go to hear the catchy, punchy, subtle, or silky-sweet lines that make movies quotable.

8. The protagonist must inevitably find him worse off at the end of the act than he was at the beginning. He must be at a crisis point. What the hell should my main character do now? That decision affects everything and always leads to . . .

9. Your antagonist must have a clear master plan or agenda. Many times we will take the time to clarify the goals, needs, and desires of our main character, but we'll fail to clarify the same for our antagonist. Your story is only as good as your baddie, so don't forget to flesh them out. In fact, many stories with problems result from antagonist issues. If you know the complete agenda of the bad guy, what he is trying to achieve and why, you can then plan the story accordingly.

Act III Goals

1. This act should feel like a headlong rush to the finish. There is no room for fluff here.

2. Make the climax the biggest moment of your film. You should know your climax before you start writing and write backward. Like a maze, which is easier to navigate if you start at the end

and go back to the beginning, the secret to screenwriting is that it's much easier if you know your ending before you start.

Let me repeat: Most writers need to know where they are going before they go there. Once the end is understood, the story merely becomes a filling in of beats that lead inevitably to this moment. And Lord knows, when you finally get to the climax, it's gotta be damn good!

3. You need a sense of resolution. Loose ends must be tied together. But the key is to tie them in a way that was not initially anticipated. If they're expecting the square knot, give them the bow, then watch 'em laugh and cry as you hang 'em. Even in romantic comedies where we know the lovers will get together and in tragedies where we know the hero will die, you must find an interesting way for the lovers to get together and for the hero to die.

4. Remember, a clear resolution is the outcome of a positive crisis decision that empowers your protagonist to succeed at the climax. Your story must force your protagonist to make the decision that illustrates character transformation and provides a stirring example of emotional growth.

5. Make sure you clearly define the rules of your world. In your movie, you need to define your world early and be consistent from then on. In other words, if you are writing a science fiction pic that takes place in the future, we need to see how people dress, relate, transport themselves, and so on from the get-go, and that cannot be altered halfway through your story. When E.T. flies at the end of that film, it is surprising, but it is not inconsistent with what we've seen up to then. That, then, is the key—consistency among defining what is and is not possible in the world you have set up, which may or may not correspond to the world that we live in.

6. Your ending must be consistent with your theme. Be very, very careful when you get close to the end. The end must be bigger than all the rest of the film. It must come as the most emotionally powerful moment of your film or else you're dead. And no matter what, the way you choose to end your film dic-

tates the theme of your tale. So if you are doing a comedy and you have everybody die at the end, you are in big trouble. A comedy entails big laughs at the climax, and in keeping with that, a happy ending. Romantic comedies entail the lovers getting together.

Beyond the act structure, there are also certain basic page numbers that correspond to story points. Please remember, these are not God-given formulaic points set in stone, but only starting points, guideposts, foundation markers to help you navigate the almost overwhelming superstructure of an entire full-length feature. They are employed most vigorously by nonwriters, those members of the entertainment industry who "develop" the hard-earned handiwork of writers. Without coming across here as too cynical, the presence of terms such as "story points" can be helpful, and trust me, the presence of these well-worn guideposts did not appear out of thin air.

Story points are the result of many bright people watching hundreds of fabulous films over the course of many years and then determining approximate times at which audiences have come to expect certain plot events. In other words, whether you subscribe to Aristotle's theories or Syd Field's plot points, both are reflecting assimilated expectations of audiences who have grown to expect a so-called classical story structure wherein the plot always turns after a certain period of time elapses. And in the end, if it ain't broke . . .

These formulas should provide support for the initial structuring of your story; however, there is always the possibility of them handcuffing you artistically. In order to avoid this problem, consider these guidelines as a sort of flexible boundary, an invisible fence. If they seem to be hamstringing you, be like Picasso, who mastered the academic tenets of light, shadow, and perspective at a young age and then spent the rest of his life deconstructing these rules.

Remember, just because act breaks are not labeled or indicated doesn't mean that they aren't there. So for what it's worth, here are some good guidelines.

ACT I: Keep it lean, mean, and tight.

Pages 1–10: Setup. Establish theme and tone; expose the heart of your picture. By page 7, I want to know what it is about.

Pages 11–25: The story must be established. Your dramatic problem must be presented. The stakes are set up, and the audience/reader cares.

Pages 26–29: The big first act turning point is introduced, and the story is turned in a new direction. Here we go, folks. Reversal. Discovery. Twist. POW! Leading us quickly to the end of ACT I. By page 29, your protagonist must experience a major turning point that sends us in another direction and changes the protagonist's life forever. This turning point must relate to the A story line. Also, the protagonist should have confronted the antagonist but of course failed, and now all the conflict, struggle, and fun really begin.

ACT II: The longest act, and the most difficult one to write. This is also the only act where you can breathe and explore characters and relationships.

Pages 30–45: The B, C, D, or subplot story lines should have been established by now. These subplots deal with the main character's relationships, not the plot itself; for instance, the best friend, the parent, the love interest that affects the A story line but is not the driving force of the story.

Every ten minutes or every ten pages, I WANT ACTION—*boom-boom-boom.* Never let up. Always keep building, especially in action/adventure scripts. You always have to top yourself. In ensuing scenes, the audience believes there is no way the main character can get closer to death and still escape, but the writer always seems to find a plausible way out for the main character. Here is where you can slow down a bit to explore characters, but be careful you don't slow down too much.

Page 60: The midpoint. Usually a high note that can only lead to a low note by the end of the second act. We can take a breather here, but we know it won't last for long. Exhale, and here we go again.

Pages 61–87: All that has been building up in Act II now starts to crumble. Subplots come into play and may even play themselves out, all pushing the main character down to his or her lowest moment.

Pages 88–90: The second act turning point—the major turning point for the protagonist, who should now be at his or her lowest possible moment . . . and THEN has a realization (the "ah-ha") that leads him or her to pick themselves up by the bootstraps and rush headlong into the third act. This turning point affects the course of the rest of his or her life. It is a galvanizing moment, an essential plot point when the main character realizes something about herself or her world that she did not know before, and this epiphany changes everything. Our hero finds the courage to confront something she has never confronted before.

ACT III: A series of actions in which the loose ends are tied together, always building, rushing toward the climax.

Pages 91–109: Here we have lots of cool, fast-paced scenes that push the story to the climax, involving the resolution of many subplots and building to one final resolution that is the biggest of the whole story.

Pages 110–114: Final jeopardy. Everything comes to a head here. No more uncertainty. Usually a heightened experience. The main character and the antagonist have it out and resolve the dramatic question of the story.

Pages 115–119: Epilogue. Now, get out fast.

Page 120: FADE OUT. THE END.

With these structural signposts in mind, you should be more than ready to dive into the following scene-o-gram. However, before you do, check to ensure that your script looks professional. These days with spell check and the rest, there just is no excuse for typos. I can't stress how important it is to read your script thoroughly before

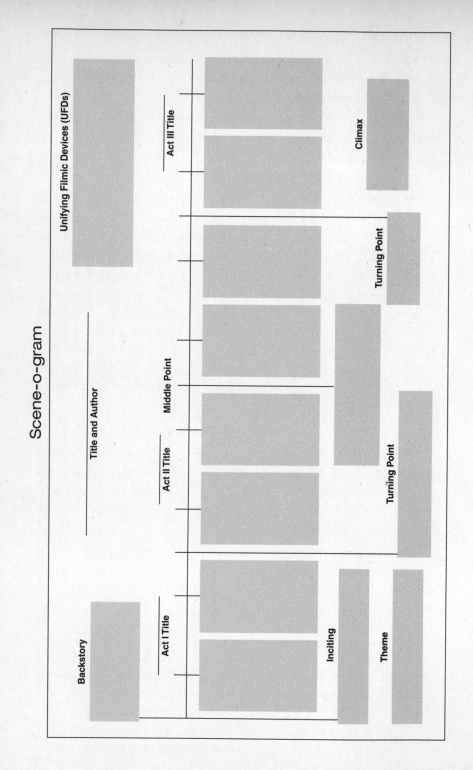

Scene-o-gram

you send it out into the world. Studio and agency readers go through hundreds of scripts a year, but believe me, if there's one thing they always notice, it's an overabundance of typographical errors. Also, avoid formatting errors. The most important thing is that you need to CAPITALIZE THE NAME OF ALL CHARACTERS when you first introduce them. In addition, pay close attention to your slug lines. If the camera needs to move to a different location, you need a new slug line. You should never have a paragraph that exceeds five lines. In most cases, they should be somewhere between one and three lines long.

Step 5: The Step Outline

Now that your scene-o-gram is complete, you should have a clear picture of the major moments in your movie and how it breaks down into three acts. If you are confused by all this crazy Hollywood ter-minology, let me slow down. As you already know, screenplays are broken down into three acts; these three acts are constructed of a series of sequences that are comprised of scenes and these scenes are then composed of beats that are then made up of lines of dialogue and action or shots. Phew! Now breathe and read that line all over again. Okay, if you've got that, we're ready to move on.

So, then, the next step involves adding the surrounding scenes not found in the scene-o-gram but still necessary to fleshing out and finishing the story. In order to do this, screenwriters traditionally used three-by-five note cards that were numbered sequentially. On the front of each card, screenwriters would write a few sentences detailing the major action that was to take place in that scene. Then they would pin these numbered cards onto a corkboard and survey their masterpieces as a whole. Rumor has it that Fannie Flagg, the author of *Fried Green Tomatoes*, would go so far as to hang her note cards on a clothesline in her basement and scrutinize her entire story. I also know writers who buy long stretches of butcher paper, hang them on their walls, and jot out every scene.

These days, with the rise of technology, you can simply enter each scene description into your computer in the form of a rudimentary step outline. The convenience of using your computer is that when all the scenes are finally lined up in the right order (and preferably written in Final Draft or Movie Magic formatting software), you need only just add dialogue and voilà, instant first draft of your script.

The step outline (AKA the master scene list) should include at least fifty major scenes—fifteen in Act 1, twenty-five in Act 2, and ten in Act three. All these scenes should be essential to furthering the story. Each should have a *raison d'être*, and there should be some change in the script's status quo by the end of every scene. As you journey from scene to scene, think of alternating between zeniths and nadirs, high and low moments, happy and sad, interiors and exteriors.

The quality and order of these numbered scenes, these Lego blocks of visual storytelling, will determine whether your script really works or not. So, then, let us begin by examining the nature of scene work, and who knows? If you can make all your scenes rock and roll, your screenplay might just take off and make you rich and famous.

Below, please find the most frequently asked questions about scenes.

#1—*How exactly would you define a scene?*

When I speak of scenes, I'm not talking about establishing shots or drive-by shots, but filmic moments that take place in one setting or maybe even in contiguous settings like the famous *Goodfellas* shot of Ray Liotta and his date going the back way through a crowded club to get to his reserved front-row seat. In fact, this famous shot is merely one part of a larger scene that continues once he and his date have sat down.

#2—*Are there any rules for the number of scenes?*

No, the only rule is that you need enough scenes to fully tell your story (although I would try not to do less than forty or more than one hundred). Romantic comedies tend to have fewer scenes than action/adventures. Also, even though it is good to number your scenes in the step outline, it is not necessary to number your scenes in your screenplay unless you are writing a final draft/shooting script. In fact, after analyzing three of my favorite films of all time, *While You Were Sleeping, City Slickers,* and *Stand by Me,* I found that none of these movies had more than sixty true scenes. However, these are all relatively short films, and they also lean toward comedy/talky genres. In essence, probably the only cardinal rule of scene work that cannot be denied is simply this—GET INTO THE SCENE LATE, AND GET OUT OF THE SCENE EARLY! It is imperative that you don't dilly-dally. Start the scene as late as possible and end it as quickly as possible. No need for "Hi" and "How are you?" or for long good-byes.

#3—*How do I know if I need a particular scene?*

The key understanding you must have of scene work is simply that every scene must necessarily have its own raison d'être. If the scene is funny but doesn't push the story forward, sorry, Dostoevsky, but it's gotta go. Yes, Fyodor, there's no room for self-indulgence in screenwriting, the most densely rigorous of writing genres, excluding haiku and those wacky limericks.

#4—*But how do I know what scenes to include and in what order?*

Good question. An answer might be found in conceiving a new way to think of scenes. Imagine each of your scenes as billiard balls on a plush green flat pool table; when you roll one ball into another, action ensues. That action is not frivolous, but a direct result of the preceding movement. This, then, is the key to understanding scene juxtaposition. As in Newtonian physics, for every action there is an equal and opposite reaction. All your character's actions have specific ramifications on the other characters within the text as well as on your story as a whole and on your audience. In movies, everything is linked. SCENES ARE RULED BY CAUSALITY.

Yes, many things in real life do happen arbitrarily, but not in the world of screenwriting. In fact, my students receive a poor grade if they dare to have a coincidental incident occur after Act I of their scripts. Coincidences are a sure sign of lazy storytelling, and good storytelling is not for lazy people. With this in mind, it becomes clear that for the climax of your story to be reached, a series of scenes must occur in a certain order that is, in retrospect, inevitable. So, like billiard balls, one scene rolls surely into another, setting off a chain reaction of seemingly inevitable events that you as the godlike creator of this world have initiated. . . . And there are still folks in Hollywood who believe that writers aren't incredibly powerful people.

#5—How do I know when a scene is finished?

You must never lose sight of this simple fact: SCENES ARE SHORTHAND! In dense psychological novels, we can digress into the minds of our characters and deal with esoteric backstory information, but in movies, we can't. So we must give basically everything we need to know about the character in the first scene in which we meet that character. Scenes work quickly, images are powerful, and first impressions are lasting ones. Thus, when you introduce a character in a scene, you are basically getting a page, or one minute, to let your reader and audience place them in their minds. Of course, you can complicate the character further on in the script, but there just is not time for lengthy diatribes. Therefore, most characters fall into archetypal patterns, and we readily accept those patterns.

#6—Can you be a little more specific there, Professor?

Of course, let's go back to the big three films I mentioned earlier. Let's start with *City Slickers*. In Act I, which lasts only twenty-eight minutes, there are really only seven true scenes. Scene 6, the party scene, serves as a mirror of Billy Crystal's crumbling life. It allows for Scene 7, where his wife urges him to go find his smile. In essence, she is telling him to go enter the second act, go on that trip to the Wild West. His turning point, his decision, takes place in his mind at the very end of the scene when the camera zooms in on his massive forehead, and then we cut to the Wild

West and the music rises powerfully. Later on, the end of Act II occurs at Scene 29 (eighty-five minutes) and the climax occurs thirty-five scenes (ninety-eight minutes) into the film. There is a long epilogue in the film, and we wrap up a few scenes later. All the fun ends after only thirty-nine scenes and 105 minutes.

In *Stand by Me*, Gordie, the main character (Richard Dreyfuss as a young man), decides in Scene 17 (thirty-one minutes into the film) to trek forward to find the dead body. The end of Act II occurs at Scene 30 (sixty-eight minutes), and the climax occurs thirty-three scenes (seventy-eight minutes) into the film. However, this is a short film that only lasts eighty-four minutes in total and is comprised of thirty-seven true scenes.

In *While You Were Sleeping*, it takes Sandra Bullock fourteen true scenes (twenty-three minutes) to get to her turning point, where she finally decides to continue the charade of being the comatose guy's fiancée. The end of Act II occurs at Scene 41 (sixty-six minutes) and the climax occurs fifty-one scenes (ninety-eight minutes) into the film.

#7—*So what's it all mean?*

In a nutshell, you should now see that there are no hard and fast rules about scenes except for these four reminders . . .

1. Get into the scene late, and get out of the scene early!
2. Each scene needs its own good raison d'être.
3. Scenes are ruled by causality.
4. Scenes are shorthand!

Obviously, every movie has a different number of scenes, especially considering how you count what is a true scene. No matter how many scenes you end up with, simply put, if you choose the right combination of scenes, juxtaposed together in the right order, never losing sight of the fact that each scene must push the story forward while combining the main plot elements with subplot elements, you can create storytelling cold fusion that will explode onscreen as well as in the hearts and souls of Hollywood readers and the moviegoing public alike.

• • •

So now, with that deep understanding of scene work, look at your original source material again. You can't use it all and you might have to make up some scenes, but in the end, your only job is to visualize the fifty or more crucial scenes you need to write your adaptation. Place them in order in your step outline and see if they work. When you think you have captured every single necessary scene and placed them in the right order to make your screenplay work, your step outline is finished.

Congrats. Now, go to script. AMEN!

3

Legal Issues of Adaptations

This entire book is dedicated to taking work from an assortment of different mediums and making it fly as a screenplay. However, before you even begin pondering what story you want to adapt into the next Academy Award–nominated script, let us first approach the issue of underlying rights. If you are basing your movie script on Homer's *Odyssey*, a historic event, or a published manuscript that is more than seventy-five years old for which the estate has not renewed the copyright, you're in luck. This is the realm of public domain material, which means material that, in terms of rights issues, is free and clear. So, hip, hip, hooray, feel free to disregard this chapter and go straight to the next.

However, most writers I meet tell me of a book they recently read or a living person's story that they want to transform into a script or even an article they saw for which they want to acquire the underlying rights. In these cases, it is silly to start doing Professor K.'s five-step process before you've dealt with contractual issues that might, if not handled carefully, impede you from ever getting the rights to the material. Simply put, before you go any further and waste time on a script you might never be able to shop around, check out the legalities. Although I am not a lawyer, I've played one on TV, so I feel that I can give you valid advice here.

Actually, I've never even played a lawyer on TV. The following advice and forms are merely starting points for optioning materials and life rights. I would strongly advise that you consult with an entertainment attorney and have him review any material you might want to use before you spend a great deal of time developing your screenplay. The documents included in this chapter are merely boilerplate legal releases I have used to secure rights for adaptations, and I make no claims for them to be perfect, all-inclusive, or legally binding. However, they have all been reviewed by a bona fide entertainment attorney, and they've worked for me.

With that said and all those nasty legal qualifiers now behind us, let's get to it. You've met someone who has an amazing life story and you want to write the script. What do you do now? I iterate and then I'd like to reiterate, do not just start writing. You have a choice. You can change her story and all the names of the people involved and just write your own version, which one might label INSPIRED BY A TRUE STORY or SUGGESTED BY TRUE EVENTS. The other way to go is to do the work to secure the life story rights from the person and advertise on the cover of the script that this screenplay is BASED UPON A TRUE STORY or BASED UPON TRUE EVENTS. What are the costs and benefits of each scenario?

First of all, if the person is not famous and his name does not carry a recognition factor, you might not even want to bother saying that it is inspired by a true story or dealing with rights issues. Instead, just make sure that you change around enough names, settings, and events to ensure that you are not clearly portraying living people who may sue you, especially if your story makes huge vats of money.

Yet there is something to be said for projects that have rights attached. In fact, many times sales of scripts happen because the writer has exclusive rights to a person's story. So there is value in having rights. If it is important that this tale be the true story based upon a person's life and use real names or if the story's characters and circumstances are so unique that you don't want to write around them, you might best be served by acquiring the rights.

The following letter is one I have used in the past to secure rights. Obviously, it is just a starting point, but it is better than nothing. Also, it is written for someone who does not have a lot of money to spend on optioning material. People think screenwriters are all rich and that everybody associated with the movie business has millions. So make it very clear that what you are offering is not a big-money deal, but your time, services, and energy. To hire a Hollywood sceenwriter to do the script, they would have to lay out $50,000 to $500,000, while you are willing to write it for free, they get a finished screenplay, and as a bonus, you are paying them for the rights to do all that work.

They will get more money down the road when the movie goes into production, but assure them that there is usually not big money involved and that even if a movie makes millions, most of that money goes to the producers and the distribution companies So for get the money and let's get that story out to the world. In addition, if you are dealing with an author, don't forget to reassure her that once the project gets made, book sales will skyrocket. Homer Hickham, author of *Rocket Boys*, didn't have a best-seller on his hands until the movie version of his autobiography came out, *October Sky*, and then boy, did it sell a lot of copies.

RIGHTS LETTER

April 1, 2003

Richard W. Krevolin
1 Hollywood Plaza
Lala Land, CA 00000

Re: *The Incredible True Life Joe Blow Adventure Story*

Dear Joe Blow:

It was a pleasure to meet you and I am very excited about the prospects of working with you on your life story. After spending time talking with you and reading your book, I do believe we have a very valuable and workable [stage play, documentary, or film screenplay] concept, and I would very much like to move forward developing and writing it.

Upon signing this agreement, you hereby give me the exclusive right for one year starting April 1, 2003, until

April 1, 2004, to try to develop a stage, documentary, or film project based upon your life story and more specifically your life as an incredibly cool _____. It is also understood that if there is bona fide third-party interest in the project at the time of April 1, 2004, and still no deal, you will extend this option for one more year.

It is understood that only $1.00 (one dollar) is being paid at this time, but we will enter into a more formal agreement reflecting the money you should receive for the rights to your story when the story is optioned or sold to a production company.

I believe that this covers our full understanding and by affixing your signature hereto, and to the original duplicate of this letter, it shall become our entire agreement.

_____ DATE _____, 2003
      Richard Krevolin

AGREED TO

_____ DATE _____, 2003
      Joe Blow

Here is an alternative letter I have used that comes equipped with a basic deal memo that should be signed in conjunction with the cover letter. This is a little more specific and can be a safer bet than just putting all the money and business stuff off until a later date. However, the deal memo is still rather limited. It is just a basic letter of agreement that is simpler than a contract, but functions like one. So if things heat up with your project, you will need a complete and lengthy agreement form written by an entertainment lawyer that will consider all the potential areas of negotiation and remuneration that may arise.

COLLABORATION AGREEMENT

April 1, 2003

Richard W. Krevolin
1 Hollywood Plaza
Lala Land, CA 00000

Dear Joe Blow:

This letter is intended to clarify in writing my desire to develop, write, and try to market a screenplay and/or teleplay based upon your novel, *Joe Blow's Incredible Adventure*. I am not wealthy enough to put big money down to secure an option. However, I am willing to dedicate the next year or two of my life to writing the script to your fantastic book and working to get it made as a movie, cable movie, TV movie, or TV series. But before anything happens, there must be a script.

As in life, there are no guarantees, but your passion and love of this material have inspired me to take a chance and write this script. In other words, if you give me a chance, I know I can write a beautiful story that will make you proud. I will be doing all this on my own time and purely with money out of my own pocket, so I hope you understand why I cannot offer you the big money you deserve to secure the rights to your story.

Hope to hear from you soon.

All my best,

Rich Krevolin

P.S. Enclosed please find a more formal deal memo.

DEAL MEMO

April 8, 2003

Re: The *Joe Blow's Incredible Adventure* Screenplay

Dear Joe:

It was a pleasure meeting with you and I am very excited about the prospects of working on the *Joe Blow's Incredible Adventure* screenplay. I would very much like to move forward developing and writing it. However, first, I feel it is important for us to clarify everything in writing, so please find the basis of our agreement outlined and reduced to writing below.

(1) <u>Time Period</u>—Upon signing this agreement, you hereby give me the exclusive right for two years starting May 1, 2003, until May 1, 2005, to develop and market to TV, cable, and feature film mediums a screenplay based upon your novel, *Joe Blow's Incredible Adventure*, for the fee of $1.00 (one dollar). It is also understood that if there is bona fide third-party interest in the project at the time of April 1, 2005, and still no deal, you will extend this option for one more year.

(2) <u>Credits</u>—Whenever the screenplay is produced and under whatever title, the writing credit shall read as follows: "Screenplay written by Richard Krevolin, Based upon the novel by Joe Blow."

It is understood that we will enter into a more formal agreement reflecting these terms and other customary terms and conditions, including of course the money you should receive for the rights to your story (all subject to good faith negotiations), at such time as there is interest in the finished script.

I believe that this covers our full understanding and by

affixing your signature hereto, and to the original duplicate of this letter, it shall become our entire agreement.

_____ DATE _____ , 2003
      Richard Krevolin

AGREED TO

_____ DATE _____ , 2003
      Joe Blow

Once you have optioned material and you want to renew that option, please use the following letter as an example of a proper renewal form. However, unless you have written into the contract that you have the unilateral right to renewal, Joe Blow is not obligated to accept this renewal, unless, of course, there is bona fide third-party interest as stated in the contract.

April 15, 2003

Richard W. Krevolin
1 Hollywood Plaza
Lala Land, CA 00000

Dear Joe:

The purpose of this letter is to inform you that Richard W. Krevolin ("Producer") elects to extend your option to purchase the Life Story rights and to obtain a commitment to produce a motion picture photoplay based on a screenplay written by Richard W. Krevolin based on the true life story of Joseph Blow ("Owner"), from January 1945 to December 1951 (the "Life Story Rights"), for the first one-year period commencing on October 9, 2005, according to the original Life Story Rights Agreement agreed to and accepted on October 9, 2003. The screenplay, previously known as *Joe Blow's Incredible Adventure*, is presently entitled *Anyone for Cheese and Monkey Mauling?*

Also, according to the October 9, 2003, original agreement, enclosed is the payment of an additional One Dollar ($1.00) necessary to extend Owner's one-year option through October 8, 2006.

Sincerely,

Richard W. Krevolin

Let's say you know a few people in that wacky world of business that we call show. You also believe that there is a great piece of material that would be just perfect for your Hollywood contacts, but you want to protect yourself from bringing that material to them and then having them go directly to the owner of the material and cutting you out of the deal. Which many Hollywood folks would do in a second, even if they are related to you and you used to be the best of friends. So what do you do?

Why, you put together a shopping agreement with the person who has the rights to the material. Once you have a signed shopping agreement, you should feel safe to market the material to your contacts, and you will be guaranteed a piece of the action if the deal moves forward. Also, this might be of use to you as a writer if you want to have a piece of paper that binds you to the person who is showing your material around town.

SHOPPING AGREEMENT

October 29, 2003

Re: *Joe Blow's Incredible Adventure* Screenplay

Dear Richard Krevolin:

This agreement ("Agreement") dated as of October 29, 2003, is entered into by Biggy Conman ("Producer"), on the one part, and Richard Krevolin ("Owner"), on the other part, with respect to the proposed development, production, distribution, and exploitation of one or more motion pictures based upon/inspired by/relating to the screenplay written by Owner entitled *Joe Blow's Incredible Adventure* (the Project). The parties agree as follows:

1. In consideration for the efforts by Producer to obtain financing for the Project, and other good and valuable consideration, upon the signing of this agreement by Owner, Producer hereby acquires an exclusive right to submit and represent the Project to motion picture studios, television networks, and other potential financiers (collectively, "Financiers") to solicit their interest in optioning, purchasing, or otherwise acquiring the rights in and to the Project and in financing, producing, distributing, and exploiting the Project.

2. The term of this Agreement shall commence upon the date of this document, October 29, 2003, and continue for ninety (90) days hence, ending on Jan. 29, 2004 ("Term"). This Term shall only be extended by the term of any executed option/sale agreement with Owner that results.

3. Producer and Owner agree that if, during the Term, a Financier desires to license, option, purchase, or otherwise acquire the Project, the Owner shall negotiate in good faith the Owner's own agreement with the Financier for licensing, optioning, purchase, or other acquisition by the Financier (or its designee) of the Project. Similarly,

the Producer shall negotiate its own agreement with the Financier for services and rights to be furnished by the Producer for agreements with the Financier. The Producer's agreement with Financier will be negotiated in good faith and will be consistent with custom and practice in the motion picture industry.

4. The Producer agrees to submit to the Owner a list of all places that the material is submitted within a week of submission. This Agreement does not constitute a partnership or joint venture between the parties. It is understood that both the parties will enter into a more formal agreement with the Financier if there is interest. Until such time as a more formal Agreement is signed, if at all, this Agreement will be binding. This Agreement may be signed via facsimile.

5. Please acknowledge your acceptance of the foregoing terms by signing the space below.

AGREED AND ACCEPTED:

_____   _____
     Biggy Conman   Richard Krevolin
      "Producer"   "Owner"

_____

If you are writing the script in collaboration with the person who owns the rights or another writer, here is a basic collaboration agreement. As you can see in paragraph 7, I have made this a fifty-fifty collaboration agreement, but obviously, it is up to you to determine what percentage each person will receive from all funds that filter in from the project. This agreement is a good model for all collaborations whether they are among two screenwriters or even two people who are going to work together on a novel or stage play.

COLLABORATION AGREEMENT

Agreement made this sixth day of September 2003, among Joe Blow and Richard Krevolin ("Authors")
In consideration of mutual covenants hereinafter set forth, the parties hereto agree as follows:

1. The Authors mutually agree to collaborate in the development of a screenplay tentatively entitled *Joe Blow's Incredible Adventure* ("The Screenplay").
2. As agreed upon by Blow and Krevolin, the credit line shall read:

    By Joe Blow & Richard Krevolin

3. Richard Krevolin and Joe Blow shall exclusively own and hold the literary property rights, their residual rights, subsidiary rights, and all copyrights.
4. Neither author shall make any contract with a third party in connection with this literary property that will abrogate the rights of the other or interfere with or limit in any way the sale of the literary properties under this agreement.
5. This agreement may not be assigned or transferred.
6. The authors agree to work together and cooperate with each other to the best of their abilities to produce the screenplay. It is agreed that Richard Krevolin and Joe Blow may each take on additional contracts during the course of writing this screenplay. However, each party will ensure that all deadlines are met. The parties hereto agree not to participate in the writing or publication of any screenplay whose story would directly compete with this property or otherwise adversely affect sales of the book.
7. All monies, income, property, fees, and royalties derived from the screenplay, its exploitation as a motion picture, residual rights, and subsidiary rights shall be paid 50 percent to Richard Krevolin and 50 percent to Joe Blow,

based upon each party contributing equally to the writing of the screenplay. If either party fails to do so for any reason, the split of compensation will be renegotiated in good faith.

8. Authors represent and warrant that they have the full power and authority to enter into this agreement.

9. This agreement cannot be amended, except by written notice executed by all parties.

10. In the event, notwithstanding this agreement, should any party hereto breach the terms thereof, then the proceeds derived from said breach shall be held against that party in trust and as trust funds for the use and benefit of the other contracting parties in the proportions herein provided.

11. The parties agree to settle any claims or disputes arising out of or in connection with this agreement or breach thereof by binding arbitration in accordance with the rules of the American Arbitration Association in the City of Los Angeles, CA. The arbitrators' award, including cost and fees to the prevailing party, may be enforced in any court having jurisdiction thereof.

12. Regardless of the place of its physical execution, this agreement shall be interpreted under the laws of the State of California and the USA.

13. In witness whereof the parties have executed this agreement the day and year first above written in triplicate original counterparts, each of which shall constitute an original.

AGREED AND ACCEPTED:

_____   _____

Joe Blow   Date   Richard Krevolin   Date

_____

Now, as I mentioned earlier, if there is activity with the script, you will probably need to consult with an entertainment lawyer and create a more fully fleshed-out agreement. The full-length agreement your lawyer will write should address pretty much all factors, including consulting fees. Make sure that if the rights holder has certain issues with his portrayal (such as no nudity, etc.), they are clearly stipulated in the agreement. Also, please note that as technology and media change, so must contracts to reflect the new forms of storytelling that are arising. So decide what you want to present to the person you are courting for rights.

In the end, keep in mind that you are bringing something of great value to the rights holder—a potential Hollwood blockbuster screenplay—and he needs you as much as you need him.

All the best of luck with it.

4

How Faithful Should Adaptations Be?

Case Study: *Harry Potter and the Sorcerer's Stone*

There is much arcana to consider in the adaptation of novels. By their very nature, these forms are diametrically opposed to the craft of screenwriting. Film is concerned with the external, visual, and auditory representation of internal conflicts. Action and movement are the cornerstones of its foundation. The novel form is concerned with the internal, visceral, emotional, and psychological ramifications of external events. Reflection, meditation, and introspection are the mortar that holds a novel's bricks in place.

First, let's consider these entities in terms of sheer page volume. Your standard screenplay is anywhere from 100 to 120 pages filled with lots of white space. A novel can be anywhere from 250 pages to upward of 600 pages or more, and that's including very little white space. J. K. Rowling's *Harry Potter and the Sorcerer's Stone,* though not 600 pages, is still a blockbuster of a novel. It has literally rewritten the record books in terms of sales volume and has forced the *New York Times* to create another category in their best-seller list to keep Harry from dominating week after week. What was at first seen as merely a young adult novel has proven itself to have mass appeal to all ages, and it has become a true publishing phenomenon.

This, then, means that *Harry Potter and the Sorcerer's Stone* is inherently a very tricky adaptation. The novel and its sequels come to the screen with a built-in fan base of millions and millions. With this blessing and/or curse, the screenwriter, Steve Kloves, chose to write a truly faithful adaptation that barreled through the opening weekend box office record books and created a whole set of new fans for that little wizard Harry Potter.

Of course, as with any film, once it comes out, there will always be many nonbelievers, critics, and grouchy muggles. And in this case, *Harry Potter and the Sorcerer's Stone* was criticized by many as being too faithful to the novel. Whether one agrees or not with this statement, it raises a significant issue about the nature of adaptations. Is the art of adaptation about being faithful to the novel, cutting and pasting it into a screenplay, or force-fitting well written but poorly spoken dialogue into place just because that dialogue is part of the original sacred text? I think not. So yes, Virginia, there is such a thing as being too faithful.

As I have said before, adaptations are tricky, and adapting work that millions have already envisioned within their minds is obviously even trickier. *Harry* had a built-in fan base that had to be satisfied, and it had the rest of the unknowing world to enamor. It is an almost no-win situation, but somehow, Kloves seems to have satisfied many. How did he do it? Well, let's try to find some answers by closely analyzing the film version of *Harry Potter and the Sorcerer's Stone*.

I've read the novel, I've read the script, and I've seen the movie twice, and I can honestly say that Kloves has walked the tightrope and gotten cleanly to the other side. Although I was hoping for a little more razzamatazz and variation from the book, I see why he wrote such a faithful adaptation and was impressed with how well he and director Chris Columbus pulled it off. When we adapt, we're not in it to completely change the story. We're in it because something in that original work got to us, touched us, and we want other people to be touched by it, too. So we adapt it into a screenplay with the hope that those reading (and, we hope, viewing) the story we've tailored to the screen will feel what we felt reading the original material. Or, if we're lucky enough, because we're also getting paid a million cool ones to do it!

For those who say *Harry Potter and the Sorcerer's Stone* might as well have been filmed straight from the book, I say that they haven't read the book. Or perhaps they have not read it with care. There are numerous omitted scenes and lots of changes and tinkering to help the story fit the screen. Whole sections of the novel have been cut to speed up the story. The final result is not a masterpiece, but it is a truly enjoyable cinematic experience that had mass appeal. That's the name of the game, folks. And that's something *Harry Potter and the Sorcerer's Stone* has in spades.

But I fear I might be coming off too harsh here. Yes, *Harry* might not be a perfect adaptation, but it does succeed on many levels. Both the novel and the film tap into a whole host of very human emotions, including a natural desire for friendship, love, family, and power. And c'mon, who hasn't wished they had magical abilities? Please, let's be honest here. How many of you tried to light a book of matches with your mind after seeing *Firestarter*? Admit it, you did. And how many tried to levitate something or someone after seeing *Phenomenon*?

Adapting a work like *Potter* is different from adapting many novels. A good writer can take just about anything out of a story and tinker with it until the story does not suffer from its omission. This was not so with *Harry Potter and the Sorcerer's Stone*. The following this book had behind it was so strong, so loyal, and so numerous that every change to the original work was subject to the most severe scrutiny.

A fan revolt would literally have ruined this film. Hmmm, let's say there are two million fans worldwide (and that is an extremely conservative estimate). Since most people don't go to the movies by themselves but bring one or two people with them, push that two million up to four million. The average of theater prices nationwide is around seven bucks. Wrangle those numbers around, figure that each true fan will see it at least twice, and you're looking at around $50 million. Now, if these people bad-mouth the film to everyone they know, the film's gonna tank. Hype only lasts through the opening weekend. If you're lucky, two weekends. Word of mouth eventually determines the longevity of a film and thus its revenue-generating potential. You get the point. If the fans don't like it, the movie's doomed. When the movie costs $100 million to make, you just can't afford to alienate your core fan base.

But the fans loved it, your average moviegoer loved it, and millions of tickets were sold. Thus, from a financial standpoint, the adaptation was a success. There were a lot of critics who harped on it, but how many movies have the critics loved that tanked? It was a good film. I saw it twice, not because I knew I'd be writing about it, but because I wanted to see it again.

With that said, the question now still remains, Where do you, as the adaptor of a novel, start? How do you condense so many pages into so few? What do you cut? There's no precise method to use when you pare down material, but there are some good places to begin. Seek out the scenes that can be removed without having a domino effect on the rest of the story. Certainly these scenes add to the novel, but onscreen, they belabor the issue.

In the *Potter* film, the Dursleys and Harry go straight from Number Four, Privet Drive to the abandoned lighthouse when the letters from Hogwarts won't stop coming. In the novel, they try several different venues before they end up there. First they move Harry into Dudley's second bedroom, hoping the letters will not find him there. Harry tries to intercept the letter at the door, but Uncle Vernon has camped out there for the night. Uncle Vernon tries boarding up the place, but the letters keep coming. He decides it's best for them to go somewhere else. They're off to the Railview Hotel. Letters find them. Then it's off to a shack on a rock in the sea. There, as in the film, Rubeus Hagrid delivers the letter to Harry.

The bedroom move was cut, the hotel move was cut, time was condensed, and little persnickets of detail were nipped and tucked along the way. And well they should have been. This is the first act, no fluff allowed. This isn't just a rule of adaptation, it's a rule of screenwriting in general. You've only got about thirty pages to set everything up. Establish your main characters and the supporting cast, ground the audience in the world where your story takes place, introduce the dramatic problem, and move into the second act. That's a heck of a lot to cram into thirty pages. That means taking the first sixty pages of *Harry Potter and the Sorcerer's Stone* (the novel) and paring it down to less than thirty screenplay pages. So even if you want to, you just can't have lengthy scenes with Hagrid cooking sausages and staying overnight.

None of these cut scenes posed a domino effect problem to the story. I mean, c'mon, think about it. So what if the Dursleys don't stop at the hotel? Does the film really suffer by not having it? It's a stopping point and would just slow down the film. We get the end result without having to include every little piece of information. The tone is maintained, nothing is truly lost from the story, and we move forward.

Another chunk of story lopped off the Potter body was the sub-plot involving Hagrid's dragon, Norbert. This actually occupied quite a bit of space in the novel. Ron Weasley's older brother, Charlie, sends some friends to get the dragon before it is taken away from Hagrid or worse. Harry and the gang have to get Norbert to the highest tower at Hogwarts. It was a great little sidebar in the book, but in and of itself it would contribute nothing to the film and thus was not used. It's a sequence that could be removed without any consequence to the A story line.

The key thing that wasn't removed from the book was the magic. Yes, there is magic in *Harry Potter and the Sorcerer's Stone*. Not only three-headed dogs, dragons, spells, curses, and potions, but a real magic, a magic that we search for every time we go to the movies: the magic of escape, escape from all the stress of our jobs, families, traffic, and financial woes. Harry Potter is in part such a fantastic character because he personifies this need for escape. His parents are dead, the family he lives with treats him like dirt, and good lord, he lives in a cupboard under the stairs! If there's anyone who needs to escape, it's Harry Potter.

Harry has the chance to find out what we all want to believe about ourselves, to live every person's dream, to discover that we're something more than what we are, something bigger than the life we've fallen into, someone with a destiny. Magic is in Harry's blood, and his birthright courses through his veins. His life with the Dursleys has not been a pleasant one, but it has taught him to be humble. This is a hugely important character trait that allows him to deal with his newfound stardom when he discovers that he is known far and wide throughout the magical world he enters. He is famous for being the only person to ever survive the dark magic of the wizard Voldemort, an evil wizard so feared that most dare not even speak his name and instead he is just called "You know who."

Now let's look at how Professor K.'s Big Seven apply to *Harry Potter and the Sorcerer's Stone.*

1. *Who is the main character?*

   Harry Potter. He's made it to Hogwarts and now his quest will begin.

2. *What is it that Harry wants/needs/desires above all else?*

   Harry wants a family. He wants his mother and father back. He sees families all around him, children with parents who care about and support them. For all intents and purposes, Harry is alone in the world. What this boy wants is made perfectly clear as he looks into the Mirror of Erised. Professor Dumbledore, the Hogwarts headmaster, tells Harry that men have been driven to madness looking into that mirror, that they've wasted away to nothing sitting in front of it. Harry understands. Harry doesn't get his parents back, but he does find a family in Ron, Hermione, and Dumbledore, who serves as a father figure to him. Once he arrives at Hogwarts, he meets people who care about him (unlike his only blood relatives, the Dursleys), people who support and worry about him.

   Harry's need for family is his driving force in the novel, and it's his driving force in the film as well. As a writer, if you've constructed your story correctly, the hero never gets what he wants in the way he expects to get it. Such is the case with Harry. He certainly knows he wants a family, but the more immediate problem is that of the return of Voldemort, the dark wizard. It is through Harry's quest to stop him that he finds his family. Our heroes can get what they truly desire only if they put the welfare of others above their own. Keep that in mind, we'll be coming back to it.

3. *What keeps Harry from achieving his goals?*

Well, the initial obstacle is Harry's guardians, the Dursleys. This family is the kind of people we love to hate, but Harry doesn't hate them. He doesn't like them very much, but he does seem somehow incapable of hate, almost as if he is above those petty feelings. The Dursleys have spent their lives trying to keep Harry from becoming a "freak," which is the term Mrs. Dursley uses to describe both Harry and his parents. The Dursleys could have been a family to Harry, but their jealousy and fear kept them from caring for the boy.

Once Harry's out of the Dursleys' clutches, he has himself to contend with. He sees all the other students at Hogwarts and the lives of magic they lead. All the while, they recognize him and treat him as if he is special. New to magic and completely unsure of himself, all this attention only leads him to wonder how he can ever hope to live up to everyone's expectations. Even Ron Weasley knows more about Harry's own past than he does. Harry has to find his self-confidence if he's ever going to succeed. He has to let his longing for his parents go, accept who he is, and embrace his new family of friends. On some level, he's afraid to believe in himself. He's been treated as though he were nothing for his entire life, and it's hard for him to shed that skin.

My favorite antagonist in this story is the spoiled, arrogant, Draco Malfoy. Draco is everything that Harry does not want to become. He is cruel, aloof, and condescending. He is more of a foil to Harry in the novel than he is in the film, but his presence serves the same purpose in the film. He gives Harry more of a reason to succeed. It's more satisfying to prove our worthiness to our enemies than to our friends. Draco is involved in a very nice example of how a scene from a novel can and should be altered to make it more cinematic.

This scene takes place when the Gryffindors and Slytherins have broom lessons. The first half of the scene is pretty much the same in the film as in the book. Neville crashes, Malfoy steals his Remembrall, and Harry flies into the air to get it back for him. In the novel, Malfoy throws it at the ground and Harry catches it just in time. In the film, Malfoy chucks it and Harry catches it just before it hits Professor McGonagall's window. Not a big difference, but visually it's much more stimulating and is a perfect lead-in for the next scene, when McGonagall comes to get him.

That day, as a rebuke, Malfoy challenges Potter to a wizard's duel that leads them to discovering the third-floor corridor. This was omitted from the film. Why? Because although it is a fun scene, the only part of it that was necessary was the discovery of the third-floor corridor. Therefore, what Kloves, the screenwriter, does is simply have a magic staircase do the work and drop Potter, Ron, and Hermione off on the third floor. It's cleaner, faster, and still provides the info we need about the third floor that is necessary to keep the story moving and coherent.

Another antagonist in Harry's way is Professor Snape, played by the fantastic actor Alan Rickman. Nobody can sneer and smirk like Rickman. Professor Snape is someone who seems bent on destroying Harry from the first time they meet. In the novel, before the big Quidditch finals as featured in the film, there is a Quidditch match that Snape referees. Harry and everyone else thinks Snape is officiating in order to make sure Slytherin wins, or worse, to get rid of Harry for good. This scene was completely cut without any real ramifications. It really was just a lot of time spent pushing a point that we already understood. J. K. Rowling wanted the audience to believe that Snape had it in for Potter, and well, frankly, most readers had already figured that out by then.

Later in the script, Harry, Hermione, and Ron all suspect Snape of trying to steal the Sorcerer's Stone. Snape definitely doesn't like Harry, but he is, in fact, trying to protect him. Thus Snape presents a fine example of an apparent antagonist who is revealed in the end to be an ally. Voldemort, via the stuttering Professor Quirrell, is the true antagonist who is really trying to acquire the stone and put an end to Harry.

For all the talk about how *Harry Potter and the Sorcerer's Stone* was one of the most faithful adaptations ever to hit the screen, one must admit that in many ways it's really no more faithful than any other adaptation. Yes, it may have included more particulars than most adaptations, but they were necessary to create the world Harry inhabits. The magical world created in J. K. Rowling's books is an alien realm that might exist alongside our own culture, but to us muggles it is completely foreign. Thus, we need to be spoon-fed lots of information to understand how it works.

What, then, can we learn from Kloves's adaptation? First of all, remember, when you're cutting scenes, try to avoid those that have a domino effect on the story. Find ways to combine scenes and throw in single lines of dialogue to compensate for omitted visual information. I'm not advising you to get in the habit of telling instead of showing. I'm just saying it is okay once in a while to use dialogue to convey expository information, especially if you are conscious of doing this and thus bury that exposition amid conflict.

When James Cameron was editing *The Abyss*, his director's cut was too long for a theatrical release, and thus he received a mandate that he needed to cut down the running time. In essence, he had to do a shorter adaptation of his own film. First, he looked for scenes that he could cut that would not change the story in its entirety. He cut them. The movie was still too long. Now he had to look for entire subplots to get rid of. There's an omitted scene where Ed Harris' character throws his wedding ring into the toilet. He realizes that isn't what he wants to do and shoves his hand in to get it out. You could have just cut this single scene if not for the fact that the toilet was filled with blue disinfectant that dyed his hand. Aw, crap, now poor James has to find all the scenes that have Ed's blue hand in them and cut them, or find a way to explain a blue hand without reshooting. A time and money crunch was in place, so Cameron did a little bit of both. It was editing genius, and a real pain in the neck.

Try to save yourself from that kind of hassle. Head these problems off before you've finished the script, lest you end up rewriting half of it because you took out one scene. The key to this is finding your theme and asking yourself if every moment of the script supports it.

Every scene cut from *Harry Potter and the Sorcerer's Stone* was a good cut. The die-hard fans will disagree, but we as writers cannot have that attachment. Professor and novelist Terry Davis, who authored the novel *Vision Quest*, which was adapted to the screen, once said, "We should watch movies in a screenwriterly way, which is to say not so much as a critic and not at all as a fan, but with the passionate, curious and inquisitive eye of a member of the craft."

Be objective, kill your darlings, and give the craft what it demands of you, and you will receive a writer's high, a satisfaction akin to winning a race or finishing a sculpture, the pleasure of finishing something beautiful. Even if you never sell it, even if no one ever reads it, you have a sprinkling of your soul on paper and the satisfaction of self-expression and creation.

This is the feeling audiences go to the theater to experience vicariously. As Harry achieves his goals through the story, the audience feels his wonder and exhilaration. We all think of ourselves as outsiders like Harry, and so, as he gains power and fame, we all revel in his triumphs.

If we want to enrapture the audience, we have to make our hero's achievements interesting. No one doubts that Harry will triumph. It's not the fact that he triumphs but how he triumphs that matters.

4. *How does Harry achieve what he wants in an interesting, unexpected, and unusual way?*

We're going to skip some of the minor victories and go straight to the meat. Once Harry, Ron, and Hermione get past Fluffy the three-headed dog, Harry, Ron, and Hermione are all tested and to survive, they must all use their strength and skills. Hermione's strength is her knowledge, her book smarts. She has read so much that she remembers the secret to how to get past the Devil's Snare. In the room with all the flying keys, Harry's broomsmanship comes into play and allows them to move forward. Next, Ron can play chess like nobody's business, and that allows Harry to get past the giant chessboard. Incidentally, this involves another change to the novel. In the film, Harry and company ride pieces. In the novel, they are the pieces. The pieces they replace get up and leave the board.

By the time we reach the climax of the film, Hermione has gone back to get help and Ron has been injured in the chess match. It is up to Harry to battle Voldemort all by his lonesome. Where Ron and Hermione could rely on their strengths, Harry is now forced to overcome his greatest weakness in order to defeat Voldemort.

Harry must embrace his magical nature and trust in himself, giving in to the instincts of his birthright and confronting Voldemort's face with his bare hands. He overcomes his fear that everyone's faith in him is misplaced. This leads him to the path of all true heroes, the road of self-sacrifice. His scar, which he thought was the result of a curse, was actually a blessing, a talisman that empowers him to defeat Voldemort. His scar represents the gift of his parents' love, which is so powerful that it can protect him and even allow him to overcome Voldemort. The love he thought he'd lost with his parents' death was, in fact, with him all along. The one thing he'd have given up anything for was actually wrapped about him and shining through him all his life. He just needed a sense of self-worth and a little coaching from Dumbledore to realize it.

5. *What is being said by ending the story this way?*

You could say that love conquers all. It would be true in the context of this story, but it would only be half of the truth. Harry prevented himself from being loved. What's said after everything has come to an end is that you cannot truly feel love until you love yourself. Maybe the only way we can realize and appreciate the love of others is to stop feeling sorry for ourselves first. That's Harry's arc. He's gone from a browbeaten, heartbroken young man to a self-confident, beloved young wizard in training.

6. *How do you want to tell the story?*

This story, like the book, is told in a standard, chronological, omniscient narrative that leans toward Harry's perspective.

7. *How have the other characters in this story changed?*

No matter how a story is changed during the course of adaptation, the arc of the characters almost always remains the same. That is to say, the natures of the characters do not change from novel to film. Their appearances might (Hermione was a bit homely, with buck teeth, in the novel but she was made cute in the film), their actions might, but their nature, their essence, rarely changes from one medium to another. In both the book and the movie, Hermione has gone from a rule-abiding bookworm to a person with friends, willing to risk her academic well-being for their welfare. She now knows that friendship is more important and more rewarding than any bits of knowledge she picks up from her "light reading."

In both the book and the movie, Ron has managed to crawl a ways out of the shadow of his older brothers. He's proven to himself that he doesn't have to compete with them, he doesn't have to be better than them; he just has to be himself.

In the end, what have we learned from the film adaptation of *Harry Potter and the Sorcerer's Stone?* For starters, it's not going to kill a movie or an adaptation to try and remain true to the original text. Sometimes (as in this case) you have to stick close to the text. Adaptation is not about how much you can wrangle and mangle the original text. There are numerous changes to the original work that are not mentioned here, but they all have one thing in common: They convert the emotion in the novel to emotion for the screen. Adaptation is about capturing the essence of the original work in another medium. Inevitably, elements will be put in and others will be left out, but the heart of the story must remain. The film *Harry Potter and the Sorcerer's Stone* still has the novel's heart and soul, and as a result, it's a joy to watch.

The Big Seven: *Harry Potter and the Sorcerer's Stone*

1. *Who is the main character?*

   The young wizard Harry Potter.

2. *What does Harry want/need/desire?*

   Harry wants to get the sorcerer's stone and defeat Voldemort. On an emotional level, he wants to be loved and have a family. He also wants to find out who he is and where he comes from.

3. *Who/what keeps Harry from achieving what he wants?*

   Draco Malfoy, Professor Snape, and most importantly, Voldemort. Harry is also hindered by his size and inexperience.

4. *How does Harry succeed in the end in an original/interesting/ unusual way?*

   Harry's scar enables his touch to be deadly to Voldemort, so that when he puts his hands upon him, Voldemort is forced to disappear. He is also aided by an indomitable spirit and sense of courage.

5. *What are they trying to say by ending the story this way?*

   Love and family conquer all.

6. *How did they tell this story?*

   In the third person, no flashbacks, no voice-over, with music used to organically accentuate themes, scenes, and motifs.

7. *How did the main character and any other characters change over the course of the story?*

   Harry learns to love and believe in himself. Hermione has gone from a rule-abiding bookworm to a person with friends, willing to risk her academic well-being for their welfare. Ron just has to be himself.

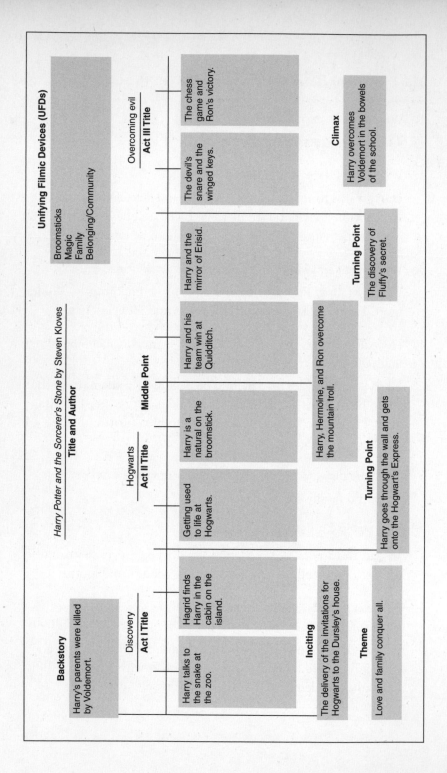

Unifying Filmic Devices (UFDs)

Broomsticks
Magic
Family
Belonging/Community

Harry Potter and the Sorcerer's Stone by Steven Kloves
Title and Author

Overcoming evil
Act III Title

The devil's snare and the winged keys.

The chess game and Ron's victory.

Climax

Harry overcomes Voldemort in the bowels of the school.

Hogwarts
Act II Title

Middle Point

Harry and the mirror of Erisid.

Harry and his team win at Quidditch.

Harry is a natural on the broomstick.

Getting used to life at Hogwarts.

Harry, Hermoine, and Ron overcome the mountain troll.

Turning Point

The discovery of Fluffy's secret.

Turning Point

Harry goes through the wall and gets onto the Hogwart's Express.

Backstory

Harry's parents were killed by Voldemort.

Discovery
Act I Title

Hagrid finds Harry in the cabin on the island.

Harry talks to the snake at the zoo.

Inciting

The delivery of the invitations for Hogwarts to the Dursley's house.

Theme

Love and family conquer all.

5

Mining the Vein and Extracting the Gold

Case Study: *The Shawshank Redemption*

There really is no agreed-upon formula used to decide when a novel isn't long enough to be a true novel and instead should be labeled a novella. I think it is up to Oprah Winfrey to make the final decision. Either way, I consulted my trusty *American Heritage Dictionary*. The definition of a novella is "A short novel." My, how helpful. It's not unlike saying that a half-gallon of milk is just a smaller gallon. For our purposes, let's say that a novella typically will not exceed 200 pages and will be more than 50 pages. Less than fifty pages, and it's safe to say we're dealing with a short story. A novella has the same intention as a novel, but generally has fewer characters and a less expansive story. A classic example of a novella would be Joseph Conrad's *Heart of Darkness*, while an example of a modern novella is Steve Martin's *Shopgirl*. It is fair to say that a novella has more of a range of characters, story, and themes than a short story, but less than a novel.

With all these definitions now behind us, the point I'd really like to focus on is simply this: If you're adapting a novel, you've got several hundred pages of material to cut. There are two or more inches of typeset pages to compress into a paltry half-inch-thick screenplay. As you're thinking about the logistics of cramming that Cadillac Eldorado into the back seat of a Dodge Omni, the novella starts looking pretty damn unadaptable. But wait, some novellas are only a mere hundred pages or so, which means you could practically cut and paste a novella into a one-hundred-page screenplay, right? Wrong. Based on the volume of prose alone, a one-hundred-page novella is roughly equivalent to 300 pages of screenplay. So put your clippers away, Edward Scissorhands, there will be no cutting and pasting today.

It's not just about cutting, it's about adding, combining, and creating. Try as you might, the more you attempt to adhere to the original material, the less your script will seem like a movie. There are lines of dialogue that just don't ring true when read aloud. There are scenes that develop character and tone but don't advance the story. You owe nothing to the original material. The goal is not to keep as much of the original story as you can, it is to make the best choices you can with the material you have in order to produce the best screenplay possible.

You always hear people say, "It's not as good as the book" or "It was so much different than the novella." But their basis for comparison is flawed. Sure, some stories work better as a novel and others flourish on the screen, but a two-hour movie can never do justice to the vast depth and breadth of a brilliantly conceived 200-page novella. (With that said, let's take a moment of silence to mourn the brilliant pieces of literature that have been bastardized on film . . . silent prayer, please . . .)

Ah, that's better. I wonder if audience members ever think, "Man, am I glad they didn't stick so closely to the book, that movie would have been eight hours long!" And so, next time your fellow moviegoer starts to complain, feel free to remind her that you are fortunate you aren't stuck there for fourteen hours to see the complete, unabridged, verbatim adaptation.

In any novella, there is a single vein from which the lifeblood of all subplots flows. Seek out this vein and extract it. Disregard the subplots dangling from it for now and just concentrate on the main character. Who is the story really about? What is his journey? Okay, now you've nailed your protagonist.

Next is the issue of the central story. Ask yourself what the point of this story is. What is this story REALLY trying to say? Find the one word that encompasses that tale. It could be hate, revenge, hope, lust, love, brotherhood, justice, anything. Once you have that word, look at your subplots. Which of these are congruous with that one word? If it's a story about revenge, chop away every subplot that is incongruous with the overriding concept of revenge. Shear them all away, but don't throw them away.

Now that you've got subplot fever, let's ride with it for a bit. Lay these subplots out on paper. Look for any that have characters in common. With any luck, one character should appear more than all the others. This character will be more intertwined with the central storyline than any other (except, of course, your main character). The other thing to look for is a narrator. If that narrator is present in the story (like Red in *Shawshank*) and not some unseen outside force, that's the character you're looking for. Either way, once you've found this individual, you've found your B story line. In any screenplay, there's an A story line, a B story line, a C story line, and so on. The A story is the central and most important, and as you creep further into the alphabet, the story lines become smaller and the characters less significant with regard to actual screen time. The B, C, and D story lines are basically a quick-reference tactic for you to keep your subplots straight.

So you've still got some subplots left, I would imagine. What to do with these? Try combining the characters you have left into necessary, preexisting B, C, or D story line characters. In other words, take a two-dimensional minor character and make him more interesting by endowing him with the qualities of another character. Now you've helped bring a major supporting character alive, maintained certain story elements that are necessary for the plot, and lost a minor character that really was only there to serve a minor story purpose and wasn't integral to the plot anyway.

You might even want to ask yourself which character's stories could be combined. It's a great way to keep the story elements intact and still cut down on script pages. Also, you should be asking yourself whether or not the remaining subplots are absolutely necessary to properly execute the central story and whether or not you have time to utilize them at all. How will you know if you have time?

First of all, determine your main character's arc. That's the next step. Now consider every element of the story and decide whether or not the story will still work without each individual element. It might be a beautiful image or a hilarious moment, but if it's not a scene that moves the story forward, it has to go. We're unwrapping Christmas presents here. We don't want the paper or the virtually impenetrable packaging the toy comes in, all we want is the shiny red fire engine inside, complete with hoses, moving ladders, and action-pose firemen.

What I mean is this: If it's not moving the story forward, it's slowing it down. If it's slowing it down, then it must be amputated from the body of the work. And when you cut, cut clean. There are always ripple effects after any edit; you must double-check the entire manuscript to make sure that it is all still in keeping with the new revisions.

We're going to plunge deeper into this subject, but we're going to do it with the help of Frank Darabont and his adaptation of Stephen King's novella *Rita Hayworth and the Shawshank Redemption*, which comes out of his collection of four novellas entitled *Different Seasons*. *The Shawshank Redemption*, for my money, is the best novella adaptation to grace the silver screen. I remember walking out of the theater and thinking that *Shawshank* was as close to a perfect film as I'd ever seen. It did not win the naked genitally challenged golden man for Best Picture, but I think it should have.

Screenwriting is a craft of decision-making, and it is by these decisions that the quality of the work is determined. The decisions Darabont made with this adaptation established him as a writer of the highest caliber. We'll start with the first step of adaptation (and indeed of screenwriting in general) and choose our main character.

In the novella, Red was actually the main character, but he was telling Andy Dufresne's story. This, then, marks Darabont's first change to this tale. In Darabont's screenplay, Andy is the main character, this is his story. Red is our narrator and a very important supporting character, but his growth is a result of Andy's, and only through Andy does he come to know true freedom. So even though it is Red's voice that we hear throughout the film, he is not the protagonist, he is merely the narrator.

It is through the story of our main character, Andy, that we learn the stories of others in the world he inhabits. *Shawshank* is a story about hope, a story about what it means to be institutionalized, a story about redemption, about will, faith, cruelty, kindness, and friendship. You could say that it's a story about good overcoming evil, but Christ, you can say that about damn near every story. *Shawshank* is a story about hope, what happens to you when you lose it, and what happens when you hold onto it. It is the story of Andy Dufresne, a man who held onto hope.

Find what it is that makes you root for the main character and magnify it. Andy is subject to a most brutal kind of injustice. He is imprisoned for a crime he did not commit, raped, beaten, and nearly broken. In this world, there is a hell and it's Shawshank State Penitentiary. There is, perhaps, nothing more aggravating than seeing the innocent punished. As human beings, we naturally crave justice and hate injustice. Thus the audience is automatically and very quickly on Andy's side. How can we not be; it is in our very makeup. So we root for Andy to receive justice and we know that no one deserves it more than him.

Ah, we've made it through the first leg of the journey. You've wrenched the spine of the story out of your novella and pinpointed your main character and his story line. Why, I'll bet you've even begun shaping that story into a screenworthy tale. Prop your feet up on the coffee table, make a nice cup of hot cocoa, and relax. Isn't that nice? Take a couple deep breaths . . .

There you go, this adaptation business isn't so tough. Okay, that's enough, put the cocoa down, get your feet off the table, and get back to work. Or you can go ahead and finish your cocoa while your neighbor finishes his adaptation of the exact same classic public-domain novella a month before you do and sells it for a cool mil. It happens, believe me.

There's an illness infecting a lot of young writers today that makes them want to have the main character in every single scene. *Shawshank* is the vaccination against this wretched virus. Secondary characters deserve their time in the limelight. This time might be best put to use as a thematic contribution. Among other things,

Shawshank brings to light the issue of institutionalization. Red said it best: "These walls are funny. First you hate 'em, then you get used to 'em. After long enough, you get so you depend on 'em. That's institutionalized."

Prison old-timer Brooks Hatlen (played by James Whitmore) is proof of Red's theory. What happens to him and what he does to himself when he gets out is a grim foreshadowing of the possible futures of Red and Andy. Darabont spends a good three and a half pages with Brooks, and only Brooks. Later, after Andy's escape, we spend time with Red, a good ten pages or so. This is as it should be. Andy's story is finished, but this is a story about hope. And there's no way Darabont's gonna leave Red in Shawshank with his hopes unfulfilled. But the actions of our main character still motivate the supporting characters and subplots. The only thing that keeps Red from winding up like Brooks is a promise he made to Andy. And it's through the keeping of this promise that Red holds onto hope and disproves his own theory. You can overcome institutionalization if you don't lose hope and maybe if you have a little help from a friend.

A quick note on Red: In the novella, Ellis Boyd Redding was a white Irishman. The fact that Morgan Freeman, a very fine African American actor, played the role led to very, and I mean very, little change as a result of this decision. In fact, in both the novella and the script, when he is asked why he is called Red, he answers, "Because I'm Irish." A good line in the novella then becomes a great line of dialogue in the script. Let that be a lesson to you: You can change anything you need to, and if you make smart changes, they only make your screenplay stronger than the original material.

So now let us explore the Big Seven as they relate to this novella.

1. *Who is the main character?*
   Andy Dufresne

2. *What is it that Andy wants/needs/desires?*
   Good question. This is one of the elements that make *Shawshank* so unique. We don't realize what it is that Andy is moving

toward, what his goal is, until the last twenty minutes of the film. Once we find out that Andy's been tunneling through the wall for the last nineteen and a half years, everything makes perfect sense. I'm getting a bit ahead of myself. Let's start earlier.

Throughout the story, there's one thing that doesn't change for Andy: He wants to be free. This desire is his major motivating force. But this isn't the only thing Andy wants. When he first arrives in Shawshank, he wants to make friends, to shape rocks, to try and simulate what his life was like on the outside. It's bad enough to be thrown in jail for a crime you didn't commit, it's worse to lose your wife, be blamed for killing her, and then be thrown into jail. Even if his wife was having an affair, he loved her and he misses her. But his life can never be the same on the inside.

His first realization of this happens when "the sisters" come into the picture. The real world is no picnic, but at least you don't have to fight to keep someone from sodomizing you every day. Andy's day-to-day routine is one of survival and fear. That's the worst kind of life, living in fear every waking moment, wondering who might be lurking around every corner, never able to let your guard down. No one can do that forever, and Darabont (as well as Stephen King) knows this. So Andy has an encounter with the toughest guard in the Shank, Byron Hadley. He wins Hadley's favor, and as a result is protected from the sisters. Here's another bit of Darabont's tinkering. In the novella, Bogs Diamond (the head sister) is found in his cell all beat to hell one morning. This is before Andy hooks up Hadley with his tax advice.

In the novella, Red speculates that Andy could have paid one of the screws to put the boots to Bogs, and notes that Bogs left him alone. The other sisters, however, are still on him. In the screenplay adaptation, Bogs really gets what he deserves. And what's more, we can see the cause and effect here. Andy makes it possible for Hadley to keep the $35,000 he's getting from his brother, and in return, Hadley takes care of Andy's problem with the sisters. Cause and effect, that's one of the major differences between the novel form and screenwriting. In a movie, after Act I, coincidence is unacceptable and speculation is not enough. We must have answers, answers that come directly from events we've already seen—causes and effects.

Back to the matter at hand. If Andy just wants to be free, why would he care about the library? After the sisters are out of the picture and Andy's in with Hadley and Warden Norton, he sees that there's still a chance to reclaim a little bit of the outside world's freedom. He can't have the whole glass, but he'll take every sip he can. Even after all that's happened to him, he's happy just to help someone get his GED. Enter our boy Tommy. Just when everything was hoppin' along fine, here's proof that Andy didn't murder his wife and her lover. Freedom is so close he can taste it. But Andy has become financially indispensable to Warden Norton. So, sorry, Andy, you have to stay, and sorry, Tommy, you have to go bye-bye—*bam, bam, thud.*

Look at this from Andy's perspective. He's damn close to completing his tunnel, but even if he does, there's still a chance he'll be caught. The information Tommy has not only removes that pressure and anxiety of being caught, but it vindicates Andy. Even though everyone in the Shank claims to be innocent, this proves that Andy actually is. He could be a free man, and Norton takes it all away.

This is Andy's dark moment of the soul. "Get busy living, or get busy dying." When we hear Andy say that, we think the same thing Red does. We think that Andy's going to kill himself. We find, however, that he chose to get busy living. Andy wanted his freedom back and everything he did worked toward that goal. Even after Norton killed Tommy and ruined Andy's last apparent chance for vindication and freedom, Andy succumbed to Norton's will so he wouldn't be moved to a different cell and have his secret discovered.

The way Darabont manipulated his screenplay away from the novella here tells you so much about how important it is to know what your main character wants. It might be a different goal than in the novella. Heck, you might even have a different main character than in the novella. Either way, you must know what your characters want on both an internal and external level, and use these desires to focus your story.

3. *Who/what keeps Andy from achieving what he wants?*

Yee-oww! What doesn't keep Andy from achieving what he wants? In the original work, there were several wardens. Each one had specific evils and different ways of running Shawshank. In a screenplay, what purpose would it serve to have several wardens go through? None. It would only succeed in depriving us of a wonderful antagonist. This is another good lesson: Never have three kinda bad villains when you can have one really bad one. Darabont took the evils of all the wardens in the novella and wrapped them up in one diabolically mean and cruel individual, Warden Norton. He's the primary antagonist, the puppetmaster who pulls the strings of Shawshank State Penitentiary. Norton knew Andy was innocent all along, even before Tommy came to him with proof of Andy's innocence. Why do I say that? Well, if you really thought someone was a killer, would you spend time alone in your office with him? Would you trust him with your bankroll? I wouldn't, but maybe that's just me.

Anyway, Norton holds Andy's life in his hands and he will not give it up. Andy has made him a very wealthy man and the longer he's around, the wealthier he'll be. As long as it's up to him, Andy's not going anywhere.

When Norton has Tommy killed, it finally sinks in for Andy: As long as Norton's there, he'll be there. There's another change. Tommy is transferred to a different prison in the novella, or at least Norton says he has been and Red as the narrator never speculates otherwise. But if you're going to make Norton's death justifiable, he's got to kill Tommy. That's really Norton's turning point. He was cruel up until that point, but once he had Tommy killed he became truly evil. Since he doesn't cross this line in the novella, Norton doesn't deserve to die. He simply resigns, a broken man.

However, in the screenplay he does cross that line, and we

feel that justice has only been served when he kills himself. I've always been of the opinion that if you're going to go for something, you gotta go all the way. Don't be squeamish, don't be worried about what people will think about you, only worry about what's best for the story. Long story short, if you're going to make a villain, by God, make a real, honest-to-goodness evil villain.

What's a great villain without a henchman? Byron Hadley is a brutal man; he has to be, he's the captain of the guard in a state pen. More importantly, he has to carry out the wishes of Warden Norton. Those at the top don't want to get their hands too dirty, so they have someone else do their dirty work for them. Hadley's not the smartest man alive, but he knows how to play the game. Do what you're told, keep the warden's name out of it, and show no mercy.

Hadley is never really a direct threat or obstacle for Andy, however. He has kind of a grudging respect for the wife-killing banker, but if the word comes down, he'll thump his skull like anybody else. This, then, represents yet another difference between the original work and the screenplay. In the novella, Hadley has a heart attack and retires. Just as it was with the wardens, there is a series of head screws. It's the same tactic Darabont used for ol' Sam Norton. Take all the head screws in the novella and combine them into one. Voilà, Byron Hadley. He deserves to pay a penance, and he's going to, in spades. When the state police haul him off, you know that sooner or later he's gonna end up in a place just like Shawshank. Needless to say, the other prisoners probably won't be that welcoming. Ah, justice.

Darabont used one antagonist to dispense of another. Namely, he used Hadley to kick the holy hell out of Bogs Diamond. The sisters had been a real problem for Andy, they probably would have been the death of him. They need to be removed for the story to progress. Once again, we're back to our key word—justice. Here we have three antagonistic forces that all meet their demise in a different way than they did in the novella. I've said it more than once and I'll say it again, you owe nothing to the original material. Here are several examples of things that changed as the original text was adapted into a screenplay.

Rita Hayworth and the Shawshank Redemption	The Shawshank Redemption
Ellis Redding is a white Irishman.	Ellis Redding is African American.
Red is the main character.	Andy is the main character.
It takes Andy twenty-seven years to tunnel through.	It takes Andy just over nineteen years.
Someone unknown pays a guard to beat up Bogs.	Hadley and Mert beat the bejesus out of Bogs to keep the sisters off Andy.
Several wardens go through the Shank.	Only one warden, Norton.
Several head screws go through the Shank.	Only one head screw, Hadley.
Brooks Hatlen is the librarian.	Brooks is the librarian and the guy with the crow.
Hadley has a heart attack and retires.	Hadley's hauled off by the police.
Norton resigns.	Norton shoots himself in the head.
Andy had a cellmate for a period of time.	Andy never has a cellmate.
Andy sets up a false identity before he goes to prison so he can keep some of his money.	Andy sets up a false identity in order to hide Warden Norton's illegal income.

(continued)

Rita Hayworth and the Shawshank Redemption	*The Shawshank Redemption*
Andy's dream is to run a motel in Zihuatanejo if he ever gets out.	Andy wants to run a charter fishing business in Zihuatanejo if he ever gets out.
Several jailbreaks during Red's time.	Only one jailbreak here, Andy's.
Ends with Red in a bus bound for the border.	Ends with Red and Andy reunited.
Tommy is transferred to a different prison.	Tommy is murdered.
The sisters keep on Andy after Bogs's beating.	The sisters stop after Bogs's beating.
Wardens made money selling drugs to inmates (among other things).	Norton's primary illegal income was from his Inside-Out program.

These are just a few examples and by no means a comprehensive list of the changes. That list would be long enough to occupy you for an eight to twelve stretch for breaking and entering. So then, let us get on to

4. *How does Andy achieve what he wants in an unexpected, interesting, and unusual way.*

We know, of course, that Andy escapes from Shawshank by tunneling through the wall and crawling through a good five hundred yards of feces, urine, vomit, and all the other lovely things we find in sewage pipes. He gets all the money from the fake accounts he set up and lives happily ever after in Zihuatanejo. Once we reach the climax, we have to go back and see how it happened. This is one of those endings that makes perfect sense as we look back on the film.

Things that at one time seemed insignificant now snap into place in the grand jigsaw of the story. By the end, instead of feeling manipulated, we slap ourselves in the forehead and say, "By God, I'm such an idiot. I should have seen that!" The truth is, we don't feel manipulated. If we did, then that would be a result of bad storytelling; in fact, we feel thrilled to see how it has all come together in a different way than we expected. Yet now that it has come together, we realize everything was pointing in this direction the whole time. We were just too blind and deluded to notice. My bad. This same kind of effect takes place in other successful third-act twist films like *The Usual Suspects* and *The Sixth Sense*.

Both of those films take some time to go back and explain the ending, or rather, to refresh the audience's memory. We see some quick flashes that explain how and why things turned out the way they did. *Shawshank*, however, takes its sweet time. It's been a patient story thus far, and there's no reason to change it now. Red has been our guide throughout the film, and Darabont makes sure that he guides us to the end. Usually films end with the conclusion of the main character's story and so does *Shawshank*, but it's Red's story as well. He's really who we're with for the last fifteen minutes of the film.

5. *What are you trying to say by ending your story this way?*

I've already touched on this several times in this chapter, but let's recap one last time. No one said it better than Andy: "Hope is a good thing, maybe the best of things, and no good thing ever dies." What *Shawshank* is saying is that you can achieve anything if you hold onto hope. Once you lose hope, though, life is over. Do not pass Go, do not collect $200.

6. *How do you want to tell your story?*

Shawshank is told using Red as a narrator. Many teachers of screenwriting frown upon voice-over narration. They do this because they are all mean, unhappy people. No, the truth is that voice-over narration can be horribly intrusive, and, VO can lead to a talky film that does not allow the audience to reach its own conclusion, instead of relying on visuals (as all films should). However, I am a huge fan of properly executed voice-over, as displayed in the wonderful work King and Darabont have done with the narration in *Shawshank*. The purpose of narration is not to tell you what's happening on the screen, but to add to that which we already know and see.

Look at it like this. There's a three-piece string orchestra filling the air with sweet music in the restaurant at which you are dining. So you and your significant other are enjoying a romantic evening, wining, dining, dancing; it's a night you'll remember forever. Or at least it's something you can bring up when your guy or gal complains that you never take them out anywhere. The waiter brings the house specialty dessert in which you've planted a beautiful engagement ring. Everything is going according to plan. Just as the waiter is setting the dessert down— SKRAAANK!

The violinist strikes the most hideous note inside the human auditory range. This in turn startles the wine steward, who trips over Old Lady Copas's oxygen tank and launches a bottle of Merlot across the room. The bottle knocks the dessert from your waiter's hands and sends two month's salary skittering across the floor.

The point is that you never would have noticed that damn violinist if he hadn't screwed up. His efforts would simply have contributed to a wonderful evening. That's what a good narrator will do, contribute to the beauty and truth of the story by adding insight and subtly accentuating the moment.

7. *How do your main character and any other characters change over the course of the story?*

Byron Hadley: Good 'ol Hadley doesn't undergo much of a change at all, but it's satisfying to know he bawled like a baby when the cops took him away.

Warden Samuel Norton: Norton becomes more and more corrupt as the story moves along. He goes from a Bible-toting hypocrite, to a man who uses his prisoners to line his pockets, to a man who has Tommy murdered in order to protect his assets. He pays his penance in the end and kills himself.

Ellis "Red" Redding: Red has already convinced himself that he's never going to get out of Shawshank. Worse yet, he feels that if he does he'll end up just like Brooks Hatlen. He's an institutional man now. With some help from Andy, he finds hope, proves himself wrong, and feels the excitement "only a free man can feel."

The Boys (Heywood, Skeet, Floyd, Jigger, Ernie, Snooze): No drastic changes here, but Andy's influence brings them closer and lets them feel a little more like human beings.

Andy Dufresne: Andy runs a full gamut of a true emotional and mental arc. Initially, at his murder trial, Andy does nothing to help himself. He displays no emotion, he does not plead for mercy or well up with tears. Any show of emotion in any direction would have helped him. When he gets into Shawshank, he's not even in denial. He doesn't break down crying or become outraged by his situation, he simply accepts it. It's only when he sees his chance to be free many years later (via Tommy's new information) that he takes a proactive role and stands up to Norton. Which, of course, results in Tommy's death and Andy's dark moment of the soul.

Andy didn't kill his wife, but as he looks back on his life, he feels responsible for what happened to her. You get the feeling that he's been thinking about that for the last nineteen years. There's only one thing to do, only one way to escape everything that's collapsed upon him, only one way to keep from being institutionalized. Escape. Leave everything behind and go to a place that has no memory. And in the end, he is finally able to do this.

And so, here are some highlights of the lessons we've learned in this chapter: Don't aim to mimic the story, aim to improve the story. Make the abstract concrete. Don't be satisfied with engaging characters, we've only got 120 pages to tell our tale, our characters don't have time to be merely engaging. Transform the characters from engaging habits to outright audience addictions, so that once they see them, they can't wait for the next dose.

Do not be afraid to make alterations to the original material. Heck, Darabont's adaptation is actually several pages longer than the novella. Find the spine of the story and select the bones you want to attach. Another author produced a framework for you, a starting point. Use that starting point as a launching pad and take off. We've all read books and seen movies and thought, "It would have been better if . . ."

That's the beauty of this process: you CAN make it better. Finished films are already beyond repair, but the novella is waiting for you. It represents your chance to take a good story and make it into a great screenplay. Off to the library with you, then, and godspeed, youthful ward.

The Big Seven: *The Shawshank Redemption*

1. *Who is the main character?*

   Andy Dufresne.

2. *What does Andy want/need/desire?*

   Andy wants to be free, to have his life back again. He also wants to persevere, to keep his hopes alive.

3. *Who/what keeps him from achieving what he wants?*

   Norton, the sisters, the Shank, his belief that in some way he did kill his wife and deserves the punishment he's getting.

4. *How in the end does Andy achieve what he wants in an unexpected, interesting, and unusual way?*

   He tunnels through the wall, crawls out through a sewage pipe, cleans out the fake accounts he set up for Norton, and heads to Mexico.

5. *What are you trying to say by ending the story this way?*

    If you lose hope, you've already died. "Hope is a good thing, maybe the best of things, and no good thing ever dies."

6. *How is the story told?*

    Chronologically for the most part, with a narrator and a few flashbacks.

7. *How do your main character and any supporting characters change over the course of the story?*

    Please see above.

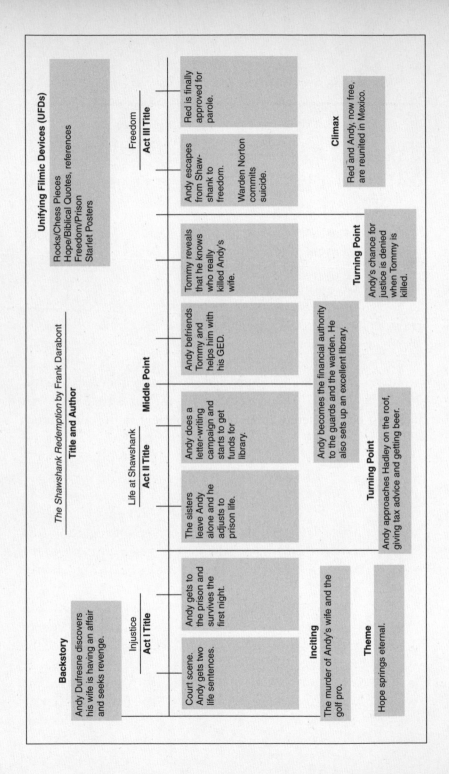

Backstory

Andy Dufresne discovers his wife is having an affair and seeks revenge.

The Shawshank Redemption by Frank Darabont
Title and Author

Unifying Filmic Devices (UFDs)

Rocks/Chess Pieces
Hope/Biblical Quotes, references
Freedom/Prison
Starlet Posters

Injustice
Act I Title

Life at Shawshank
Act II Title   **Middle Point**

Freedom
Act III Title

Court scene. Andy gets two life sentences.

Andy gets to the prison and survives the first night.

The sisters leave Andy alone and he adjusts to prison life.

Andy does a letter-writing campaign and starts to get funds for library.

Andy befriends Tommy and helps him with his GED.

Tommy reveals that he knows who really killed Andy's wife.

Andy escapes from Shawshank to freedom.

Warden Norton commits suicide.

Red is finally approved for parole.

Climax

Red and Andy, now free, are reunited in Mexico.

Andy becomes the financial authority to the guards and the warden. He also sets up an excellent library.

Turning Point

Andy's chance for justice is denied when Tommy is killed.

Turning Point

Andy approaches Hadley on the roof, giving tax advice and getting beer.

Inciting

The murder of Andy's wife and the golf pro.

Theme

Hope springs eternal.

82

6

Truth, Lies, and Alternative Structures

Case Study: *Rashomon*

In every form of art, there are those who fight conventions, Picasso and Dali, for instance, in the art world, and free-form jazz artists in the music world. They deliberately alter and contradict the parameters that others construct within their art form. By pushing the edges, they further their own careers as well as allow their art form to grow and change. But to break the rules, you must first master them. You must first be completely aware of and proficient in the conventions of your art form. Otherwise what you create is simply a confession that you do not fully understand or are incapable of working in the established forms of your medium. Like the artist who can't draw a sphere and has no concept of light, shading, or composition but can glue a pink tassel to a toilet and call it "ART," impostors are usually very talented at only one thing—hiding who they really are. And once you unmask them, these undiscovered "geniuses" prove to the world that they are undiscovered for a good reason—they deserve to be.

Akira Kurosawa was a director who was always interested in playing with conventions, especially the conventions of Western filmmaking. He was, however, a man who completely understood the art and craft of directing. Even if one does not enjoy his films, one must admire the way he used the camera. Kurosawa mastered the techniques, forms, functions, and styles of his craft. Once having accomplished this feat, he was free to spend the rest of his life exploring other structural styles.

Stop! Wait! Why are we talking about Kurosawa? Well, simply because his film *Rashomon* is probably the most famous short story adaptation of the twentieth century. It's also an adaptation that defied the Hollywood paradigm and became famous for doing so. His tale is a combination of two stories by Akutagawa Ryunosuke, *Rashomon* and *In a Grove*. *Rashomon* is a story of a servant who's out of a job, let go by his master due to a series of disastrous conditions in Kyoto at the time: "For the past few years, the city of Kyoto had been visited by a series of calamities—earthquakes, whirlwinds, and fires, and Kyoto had been greatly devastated." Bandits and thieves roam the city and countryside.

The servant in the story takes shelter from the rain in Rashomon, which is the largest gate in Kyoto, but has fallen into disrepair in recent years. He contemplates what he should do with his life. Should he find a way to earn an honest living, or become a thief? He gets cold and decides to sleep in the tower over the gate. There he finds an old woman pulling the hair from dead bodies to make wigs. She says that it's okay because she'd starve if she didn't do it. The servant rebukes her and steals her clothes, saying, "Then it's right if I rob you. I'd starve if I didn't."

Kurosawa takes little more than the setting and a few elements from this story. The famous multiple-perspective plot and structure of this film is taken not from the short story *Rashomon*, but from one of Ryunosuke's other short stories, *In a Grove*. *In a Grove* revolves around a murder trial in which each person involved tells his or her version of the tale.

The woodcutter says that he found the body of the murdered man in the forest. He's the one who reported it to the police. The priest testifies that he saw the murdered man traveling with his wife the day before. The man, he says, had a sword, a horse, a bow, and a quiver of arrows. The policeman who caught Tajomaru, a bandit who raped the man's wife and allegedly killed him, relates the story of how he captured the bandit. He found Tajomaru lying by a river, presumably thrown by the horse he had stolen, although in reality he drank some contaminated water and fell ill. The widow's mother is saddened by the loss of her son-in-law, but is more concerned with the whereabouts of her daughter (who is not at the trial yet).

Now comes the testimony of Tajomaru. He confesses to killing the man, but he does not know where the woman is. He relates how he become infatuated with the woman when the wind blew up her veil and he saw her. He had to have her, but would try to do it without killing the husband. He tricked the husband into following him, claiming that he had some fine swords and mirrors buried a little ways away. He surprised the man, overpowered him, and tied him up. He then tricked the woman into following him, saying that her husband had fallen ill. When the woman saw her husband, she attacked Tajomaru with a short sword. She fought fiercely by Tajomaru's account, but was no match for him. After he'd had his way with her, Tajomaru says she demanded the two men have at each other. "She said it was more trying than death to have her shame known to two men." So, according to Tajomaru's account, the men fought and he eventually killed the husband. The woman, however, had run off. He then robbed the man of his sword, horse, bow, and arrows, and left.

Now the widow comes forward. She had been found in a temple. Her account stated that after the rape, she could see that her husband hated her. She fainted. When she came to, there was her husband, looking at her with as much disdain as when she had passed out. She found the short sword. Though her husband's mouth was stuffed with leaves, she swore his eyes said, "Kill me." So she buried the sword in his breast and fainted again. When she awoke, she allegedly tried to kill herself in several ways, but failed. She sought refuge in the temple where the police found her.

The last testimony is that of the murdered man, told through a medium. His version is that after the rape, his wife begged Tajomaru to kill him. Tajomaru took offense and asked the husband what he wanted him to do with her. "What would you like done with her? Kill her or save her?" The wife ran off into the forest to escape. Tajomaru cut the husband's bonds, stole his weapons, and left. The husband found the short sword and stabbed it into his own breast. Just before he passed into the darkness, he felt someone take the sword from his breast.

Who is telling the truth? What is the truth? This, then, is the point of the short story *In the Grove* and the movie *Rashomon*. Both works of art deal with issues of point of view and in doing so suggest that perhaps every person's reality is different and that there is no such thing as truly objective truth. Furthermore, since Kurosawa's film is not a completely literal adaptation, the great Japanese director has altered things a bit further to add to the ambiguity.

There are obviously characters in the story *In a Grove* who are lying. What Kurosawa has done is complicate that by having those characters' stories told from yet another point of view. A woodcutter, priest, and commoner have all taken shelter under Rashomon. The woodcutter and the priest were at the trial and gave their testimonies. The commoner, however, knows nothing. Thus the woodcutter and the priest recount what they have seen and heard. Eventually the woodcutter says that all the stories are lies. He saw what really happened.

But he's already lied, so how can we believe what he has to say now? The commoner questions him about the dagger that he thinks the woodcutter stole. The woodcutter responds that the dagger was part of the reason that he was forced to lie. Although we never know for sure if the woodcutter took the dagger, there is a strong implication. The priest is losing his faith in mankind. He wonders how anyone can be believed. The commoner has simply accepted that people lie and that's the way it is.

Another nod to the original story of *Rashomon* comes when the three find an abandoned baby on the other side of the gate. The commoner steals the baby's clothes. The woodcutter is very upset about this, but the commoner says that the woodcutter is no better than he, a liar and a thief. There are parallels here regarding the original story about the old woman stealing hair and the servant's reaction. The woodcutter offers to take the child, saying that he already has six of his own and one more won't make his life any worse. This gesture redeems the priest's faith in humanity.

In terms of overall structural elements, *Rashomon* does not follow classic Hollywood three-act structure. There is no main character, there is no villain, there is no goal to seek/want/desire and thus no victory to be had. The goal of this film is not to send the audience home with that warm fuzzy feeling, but to make them think. It is not a treatise on closure and certainty, like most Hollywood storytelling, but instead is a diatribe on ambiguity and the nature of truth.

However, it can be said that the Big Seven still apply. They may not pertain to the story as a whole, but they do relate to the individual testimonies that together comprise the film. Let's take the testimony of Tajomaru, for example.

1. *Who is the main character?*
   Tajomaru.

2. *What does Tajomaru want?*
   He wants to have sex with the wife, and afterward to make her HIS wife.

3. *Who/what keeps him from achieving what he wants?*
   The husband.

4. *How does he get what he wants in an interesting/unusual way?*
   He tricks the husband, ties him up, and tricks the wife into following him back. He fights and kills the husband to try to win the woman for his own wife.

5. *What are you trying to say by ending the story this way?*
   The consequences of unrestrained impulses are greater than the reward of the impulse fulfilled.

6. *How is the story told?*
   A first-person account with flashbacks.

7. *How do the main character and any other characters change?*
   Tajomaru's change is not all that severe, but he does learn that he's not invincible. Though he defeated the husband, he was

defeated by some contaminated stream water that made him ill long enough for him to get caught. The penalty for his lesson is death, although he has no regrets.

Yes, my children, the Big Seven pertain to each of these individual tales. They apply because each of these tales has a main character and each main character has a goal/need/desire. The story as a whole does not. There is no resolution to this tale, just as there was no resolution to the short story *In a Grove*. Most popular American film, however, demands resolution. These days, one only finds this type of ambiguous storytelling in what has been labeled independent film. However, even a great majority of independent films adhere to the three-act structure and its conventions. Yet it is in the realm of independent film (which in many ways is another word for artsy, lower-budget films) that there seems to be the room, the need, and a desire for these kind of so-called "experimental films" like *Rashomon* that deal with deeper philosophical and intellectual issues.

Since it came out in 1950, *Rashomon* has been studied and adapted by scores of filmmakers. There was an adaptation in 1964 called *The Outrage* that placed the story of *Rashomon* in the Old West. William Shatner played a preacher, and Paul Newman played the bandit. The story is told by a miner and a priest to a con man in the train station where they've all sought shelter. This film is a very direct adaptation, and at times it matches Kurosawa's film shot for shot.

More recently, one can see scores of successful films that seem to owe a debt to *Rashomon*. One that blew off the doors of Hollywood and influenced a generation of young filmmakers is *Pulp Fiction*. It's a story told from several points of view with no clear resolution (by God, what's in that briefcase?). It defies the three-act structure on some levels, but not all. Each person's story has its own three-act structure. The differences here are that of chronology and narration. *Pulp Fiction* moves back and forth in time to allow Vincent and Jules to walk out of the café alive at the end of the film. A key factor in this film is that the narrator in Tarantino's movie is assumed to be reliable.

Now, as we wrap up this chapter, don't go off willy-nilly and decide to write a screenplay that defies structure, style, convention, and the principles of screenwriting simply to show how you are a true artsy-fartsy genius. I cannot stress enough how important it is to master the craft before you attempt to change it. Some people feel that because there is an accepted way of doing something, they need to do things differently. This is not a sign of genius, but merely a sign of a severe problem with authority. Go against the flow if you will, but be prepared for massive rejection.

The flow exists because it works. Hollywood classic three-act structure with a single likable protagonist is a tried and true method, a method that sells scripts. These scripts are made into films, and sometimes those films move you. Other times, they may not be very moving, but at least, usually, they are entertaining.

Sure, I know. Everyone wants to build a *better* mousetrap, but hold on there, Einstein. First, have you demonstrated to the world that you've been able to build a good solid mousetrap that has really proven itself to work?

(Due to the experimental nature of this film, its form does not truly lend itself to a scene-o-gram, and thus there will be none in this chapter.)

7

Compiling Characters, Cherry-Picking, and Captain Phenomenal

Case Study: *The Patriot*

History is a fickle thing. It's as open to interpretation as any novel or piece of fiction. Are the accounts of historical events really accurate? Who wrote down these accounts? What were their agendas? What was the author's point of view?

No human can be completely objective, and since it is we who record history, no historical account can be completely objective. Any biography is inherently biased—whether that bias might be kind or harsh—so there really is no such thing as a truly impartial biography. As for autobiographies, just forget about it. They are even more skewed. Not even the camera's eye can always see things clearly. Watch a Sunday football game and you can see instant replays from five different angles. From four of those angles it may look like the receiver got a first down, but from the fifth, it appears he was half a yard away. Who's right?

Perspectives differ, points of view change, prejudice weeds its way into the telling, and the end result is an imperfect product. There are, of course, things we know to be true and false throughout history. There are certain undeniable facts: Germany didn't win World War II, George Washington was the first president of the United States, and so forth. So we have certain points of reference to work with. You might even call them stepping stones, if you will. But we must then fill in the gaps between the stones, between what we know to be true and what may or may not be accurate. That's how biographies are written and history books compiled.

If your source material is based upon a thoroughly researched personage or piece of history that is universally acknowledged as factually accurate, then you are in good shape. That is, of course, if it is also dramatically interesting. There are many illustrations of this. *Patton, All the President's Men,* and *Thirteen Days* are all fine examples of history/biography films that did not deviate from the truth and were still interesting to watch. In fact, in the best of these types of stories, we know in the back of our minds how things are going to turn out, but we still get caught up in the action and start to question the outcome. For example, in *Thirteen Days* I knew that the Russians would not get into a nuclear war with the United States, but I was still so caught up in the dramatic tension of the Kennedy White House that I felt as if there was a slight chance that nuclear war really might occur. This, then, is an ideal scenario, one in which there are enough interesting historical facts and personages that all you need to do is pick the most dramatic ones and tell the story as it really took place, following the adaptation rules that have already been laid out in this book.

Unfortunately, most historical/biographical stories do not fit so easily into a dramatic three-act structure. Without a lot of adjusting, compressing, and twisting, most of these stories just would not make good films. Many times, they tend to be dramatically flat. In addition, often you will find that your source material will be so obviously flawed that it's almost impossible to discern truth from fiction. Looking at the subject from the adaptor's point of view, there's really only one way to minimize casualties. You must make no real claims to be portraying a definitive historical account of the depicted events, and instead you must clearly state that what you are doing is merely adapting the story into a historical fantasy.

It is a given that the Hollywood telling of a historical event will by necessity have a load of fictional elements. Like it or not, sometimes historical events just are not that dramatically exciting and need to be spiced up a bit to make an entertaining movie. Without appearing to be a Hollywood apologist, I do believe that there always is—or at least there always should be—a certain amount of leeway given to that thing we call "historical truth," especially when one realizes the complexity of dramatizing any event or personage. Thus, I'm a big believer in using the label "historical fantasy" to label and define this type of Hollywood retelling of biographies and history. The film *The Patriot* is a good example of this genre of adaptation.

One of the main sources, if not *the* main source, for *The Patriot* is the book *The Life of General Francis Marion*. This text was a biography originally written by Brigadier General Peter Horry, a longtime friend who fought alongside General Marion. Horry wasn't completely satisfied that his grammar was sufficiently competent or that his telling of the story was adequate. As a result, he enlisted the help of one Mr. Parson M.L. Weems to give it a good once-over. Upon seeing the finished result, Horry sent Weems a letter concerning his revision that, among other things, said, "You have carved and mutilated it with so many erroneous statements that your embellishments, observation and remarks, must necessarily be erroneous . . . Can you suppose I can be pleased with reading particulars (though so elevated, by you) of Marion and myself, when I know such never existed."

It's safe to say Horry wasn't doing backflips when he saw the extent of the liberties Weems had taken with Marion's biography. Yet it is Weems's revised version that one will find in the library today. There are even other works that directly contradict events stated in *The Life of General Francis Marion*. So what does the honest, hard-working adaptor do?

Sure there's a potentially great screenplay here. You want to tell Marion's story, the real story of the "Swamp Fox," but you've got no idea where to start or what to believe. You don't want to look like an idiot when you present the story of Francis Marion in a historically inaccurate light.

So what's the answer? Well, if you are screenwriter Robert Rodat, you don't tell Francis Marion's story, you tell the story of Benjamin Martin, the Ghost. Ta-da! That's step one: change the names.

Change the names of everyone you can without the moviegoing public noticing. Especially if your hero is supposed to be called Francis. (Unless of course he is a talking mule.) I'm sorry, but I just can't see Mel Gibson playing a heroic character named Francis Marion. In fact, about the only name that hasn't been changed in *The Patriot* is that of Lord Cornwallis.

Although as a nation we generally lack knowledge of our country's history, it's still not a great idea to rename the commander of the British forces in the South. But you can sure rename all his subordinates. We are not striving for historical accuracy here. The original material was used as a base solution to which the writer added his own catalysts to create a story. I stress the term historical *fantasy*. No, it is not real. No, it did not happen exactly as dramatized. It is a creation based on reality. Your duty here is to resemble reality, not duplicate it.

As an exercise, take an experience that's happened in your life and give it the good ol' historical fantasy treatment. Change the names of all the major players, glorify and demonize whomever you choose, write the story the way you always wanted it to occur. Pretty fun, eh?

Sure, there are those who might call it lying, but writers don't lie, they create. The key to this genre of adaptation is to avoid tinkering with widely known events and their outcomes. If the British win the Revolutionary War, the audience just might think something's up, but good historical fantasy never goes that far. It obeys major known historical fact; it does not include anachronisms or things that feel false. It merely fills in the blank spaces of history with dramatically powerful moments that could have and maybe even should have happened.

Now that we've freed ourselves from the shackles of historical truth per se, let's dive deeper into our case study of *The Patriot*. Benjamin Martin is our main character. A person may do a lot of things in the course of his or her lifetime, but we really don't want to hear about all of them. As with any story, you must separate the wheat from the chaff. So you read through *The Life of General Francis Marion* and glean from it those instances that are the most interesting and exciting. Since this is historical fantasy, you can also feel free to take the experiences of others and toss them in the stew as well. Toss just about anything in that you like, but don't go too far. Remember, it does not have to duplicate reality, but it does have to resemble it.

The Patriot's "Ghost" (historically, "the Swamp Fox") is the pure form of Francis Marion. He's what we all want our heroes to be: fearless, honorable, intelligent, and awe-inspiring. He's larger than life;

that's the way to build heroes. That's also part of the reason why so many choose to go the route of historical fantasy when writing adaptations. If you make your character fictional and someone says, "That never really happened," you can say, "I know, Sherlock, I made it up, but what really happened isn't the point. This is historical fantasy."

There can be only one main character, but having read Marion's biography, I can attest to the fact that there were several great characters besides Marion to pick from. I suppose it just depends on which story you want to tell. Or rather, what character traits can we cherry-pick from those individuals who are depicted in the source material? It just seems like an awful shame to stick to only one man, especially one whom no one really knows, when there are so many cool cats to chose from. So what does the savvy screenwriter do? Well, if you are Robert Rodat, you combine them all into one man, Benjamin Martin. You create the *uber* hero.

The Patriot's Martin is a combination of every brave man and deed in Marion's biography. In fact, there are elements of Martin that can be traced to Marion, Colonel Daniel Morgan (famous for the Battle of Cowpens), Elijah Clark (a Georgia frontiersman and Indian fighter), Thomas Sumter (a Virginian who served in the French and Indian War, led the South Carolina militia in victories over the British, and had Fort Sumter named after him), and Andrew Pickens (who engaged in frontier warfare with the Cherokee and served under Morgan at Cowpens). In fact, some of these characters aren't even mentioned in the Marion biography, which clearly indicates that Rodat pulled from more than one text for his adaptation.

Once you've constructed an *uber* hero, then, my friends, you'll have great need for an *uber* villain, a dastardly dude who must be the opposite and yet still the equal of Martin. And if you can't find the perfect *uber* villian in the history books, what do you do? Well, you do the same thing that you did with the protagonist: You pick elements of all your favorite Revolutionary War bad guys and merge them into one. In this instance, you combine several of the officers in the Carolinas: Colonel Tarleton (known as Ben the Butcher, so called for his policy of killing surrendering troops), Lord Rawdon, Major Weymies, Brown, Balfour, and any others who might tickle your fancy.

The construction of the *uber* villian is played out in terms of specific character traits. For instance, our hero, Marion, took a certain measure of pride regarding the treatment of prisoners. To counterbalance this, it is necessary to make the villain ruthless in his treatment of prisoners. This, it turns out, was not that difficult, seeing that Marion even said that the British officers "have often been known to butcher them in cold blood." So, yes, it seems quite fitting to include this ruthlessness in the antagonist. And, in fact, in *The Patriot* Cornwallis, in order to capture the Ghost, gives the *uber* villian, Tavington (I believe this name is a variation of the name of Colonel Tarleton), leave to use any means necessary.

In reality, Cornwallis passed an order in August 1780 that gave his officers the license to use "the most vigorous measures" at their disposal to crush this American rebellion. In other words, screw this gentlemanly conduct thing and let's win this war. These vigorous measures included hanging, shooting, stabbing, beating, raping, burning, pillaging, and otherwise tormenting the populace of South Carolina.

The worst among the officers was Major Weymies. He burned and pillaged every homestead, plantation, and shack he came across. This is a man who was known to burn down houses (after pilfering all the valuables) with the families still inside. Take all the things this guy did, then add everything the other officers did, and you have the cruelest of souls, a great screen villain—our antagonist, Tavington.

Now we've got a good guy, a bad guy, and the historical backdrop of the Revolutionary War. What next? Well, we still need clarity as to our theme. What, really, is this tale going to be about? This one's got a lot going on—vengeance, love, justice, loss, freedom, hatred—but when it all comes down to it, I suppose one need just look at the title and realize that it's about patriotism—the true costs and rewards of patriotism. Perhaps it's also about the ideals patriotism serves. It's about Martin's pride in his country and how that kind of pride helped win America its freedom. And that takes us to the oldest of all stories and probably the most American of tales, the story of the rugged individual hero who single-handedly changes history.

Yes, one man can make a difference if he has the strength to give of himself for the good of others. In fact, if you watch the climax of the film closely, Martin basically affects the outcome of the entire war when he grabs the flag and urges his men out of a retreat into an attack, thus taking what looked like a sure British victory, turning it into a British loss, and literally turning the tide of the Revolutionary War.

There are faults to be found with *The Patriot*, but as a historical fantasy adaptation, it fills a need and fills it admirably. If you're entertaining the notion of delving into this genre of adaptation, I suggest you study this film and the book from which it's gleaned. Let's look at a point-by-point comparison of *The Life of General Francis Marion* versus *The Patriot* to see how the actual events were changed into what we saw in the theater.

The Life of General Francis Marion	The Patriot
General Francis Marion was known as "the Swamp Fox."	Marion's name is changed to Benjamin Martin, and he's known as "the Ghost." Not only that, but he is not a general; instead, he is given a field commission as a colonel.
Marion's nephew, Gabriel, was a lieutenant under his command. He was taken prisoner by the British and killed. The Americans later took the man who killed him prisoner and (much to Marion's chagrin) one of Marion's men killed him.	Martin has a son named Gabriel who enlists against his wishes. He is killed by Tavington, Martin's archenemy. In the final battle, Martin kills Tavington.

(continued)

The Life of General Francis Marion	*The Patriot*
Though he didn't relish it, Marion was often pushed to procure rations forcibly for his men from those who were not willing to simply give of their livestock, grain, and amenities. Soldiers have to eat. There were, however, many generous Whigs who were more than happy to help Marion and his men.	Martin and his men can always count on the generosity of the good people of South Carolina. When they need food or supplies they are able to obtain it from the wealthy Whigs in the area. Martin never forcefully commandeers supplies from anyone.
Major Weymies, born a Scotsman, was a British officer who, once he got the go-ahead from Cornwallis, proceeded to raze every home and plantation he came across. He is known to have burned people alive in their homes.	Tavington is a ruthless British officer whom Cornwallis initially tries to control, then offers increased latitude in order to catch the Ghost. Though this villain is a combination of several British officers, his tendency for burning homes, churches, and the people within these structures was probably inspired by the actions of Weymies.
Another of those British officers ranked among the ruthless was Colonel Brown. He hung a young boy as the child's mother pleaded for mercy. Then he instructed the Indians	Tavington is one brutal SOB as well. He kills Martin's young son and orders the American soldiers being cared for (who should be taken as prisoners of war) to be executed. The man

The Life of General Francis Marion	The Patriot
under his command to use the boy's head for target practice for their tomahawks. He and other officers were also noted for killing prisoners of war.	has no mercy, an attribute extracted from the likes of Brown and Weymies among others.
Marion's men often attacked British encampments while they slept. Men frequently deserted and took the road of cowardice when it came to battle. Many were as brutal and ruthless as the British officers, but Marion kept them in check as best he could. Their ranks began to solidify when their wives and children were slaughtered. Vengeance bolsters patriotism.	Martin's men are devious, to be sure, but they never go so far as to shoot men while they sleep. None of them are deserters or cowards. Their resolve is crystalline the moment they joined Martin's ranks. They kill a few redcoats as they are about to surrender, and Martin orders that prisoners be treated fairly. They employ guerrilla tactics but are never portrayed as evil or cruel. Their cause is righteous and thus the means they employ to fight off the British are equally righteous. We're given men to root for and not given any reason to question their fidelity.
The Tories were just as much a threat as the British. These Americans who remained faithful to	The Tories are not really developed to any meaningful extent. There is one American officer who joins the

(continued)

The Life of General Francis Marion	The Patriot
England out of fear or loyalty were hated more than the British. They played a very significant role in the British army and were a constant thorn in Marion's side.	British, but that is all we see. This aspect of the Revolutionary War was not brought up in the film because it would portray a good number of the people in the colonies in a bad light.
Marion had a wife and children who were alive and well. But many of his men had lost their wives and children.	Martin's wife is already dead, two of his sons are killed, and his children live with his wife's sister. This was done because the main character's plight needs to be not only equal to but greater than that of any other character.
Baron Von Stueben, a Prussian who joined Washington's camp, was assigned to train the troops in traditional military practices.	Jean Villeneuve, the charismatic Frenchman who helped train the troops, seems to be a cross between Von Stueben and Lafayette.
Captain Macdonald, one of Marion's men, was seemingly invincible. If taking on five British dragoons by himself was the shortest way from point A to point B, that's the path he took. His heroism could turn the tide of battle.	Martin takes on the attributes of Captain Scotch Macdonald. He can and does slaughter scores of men by himself. In terms of behavior in battle, Benjamin Martin probably has more of Macdonald's qualities than Marion's.

The Life of General Francis Marion	The Patriot
A soldier by the name of Jasper was unharmed during the entirety of a battle, "But upon hearing the retreat sounded, he rushed up to bear off his colors and in that desperate act, was mortally wounded,"	Though Martin is not mortally wounded, he runs off to bear the American colors (the flag) when a retreat is sounded, and turns the tide of battle. This may have been based on the heroism of Jasper or on the heroism of Morgan at the Battle of Cowpens.
Jasper and his friend Newton rescued a group of prisoners from an escort of a sergeant, a corporal, and eight men. They shot two of the guards and bludgeoned the two officers to death with the spent muskets.	Martin's extraction of his son Gabriel from a British escort is far more grandiose, but just as brutal and cunning, not to mention quite similar to this incident.

This chart obviously does not cover the entire plot, but it is more than enough for us to see how this adaptation was handled. Clearly, the various experiences and exploits of several characters are piled into one to make our hero more heroic and our villain more villainous. This is the art of the historical/biographical adaptation. A talented adaptor must have the eye and the skill to choose the right events and characters for the adapted version. The overriding idea of patriotism was used as a sieve to help filter out the incidents that didn't support the idea. That's why we don't see a lot of Toryism in The Patriot.

I hope you've latched onto what the concept of historical/ biographical adaptation really entails and are ready to move on to the Big Seven. Let's move through the questions, keeping in mind how these story elements were extracted and adapted from *The Life of General Francis Marion*.

1. *Who is the main character?*

   Benjamin Martin

2. *What does Benjamin Martin want/need/desire?*

   Initially, Martin wants to simply enjoy life on his plantation, play with his kids, build furniture, and uncover the mysteries of the rocking chair. In essence, he wants to hide from his past. There's a great lesson in character construction here. When we first meet Ben, he's not off slaughtering Indians, he's trying to make a rocking chair and, in highly engaging and comical scenes, failing. So at first we don't meet a psychotic, berserk warrior, we meet a peaceful buffoon who collapses to the ground in one of his poorly made chairs, and of course we immediately like him. Construct your hero in such a way that he is immediately appealing, and you are well on your way to writing a viable script.

   Now, let's get back to our hero. When Martin's called to Charleston, he opposes the war. Martin will do anything to keep his children from seeing the horrors of war, which he has already witnessed. He is a man who understands war and prays that his children will never see the brutality that he has experienced. But of course his efforts and attempts are futile. Once Tavington razes his plantation, he realizes that his life and the lives of his children can never return to the way they were. The only method for him to reclaim a semblance of what he has lost is to fight.

   Martin has a lot of reasons to fight, but the one that actually brings him into the fray and motivates him on a higher level is the coldhearted desire known as vengeance. This may be the greatest motivator of all.

   While love can move us to grand actions, it lacks the purpose and power of revenge. Martin isn't South Carolina's foremost patriot until his son is killed and his home burned to the ground. This is the catalyst that brings his patriotism to life.

There is only one thing that can stop a man hell-bent on revenge—death. When Tavington kills Martin's oldest son, Gabriel, Martin's resolve is crystallized further. He will kill Tavington. We, as the audience, know that he will have his vengeance or die trying.

Martin also wants his country to be free. He does not want future generations to be subject to the cruelties of the English. Once he realizes that the only way to preserve the freedom of his countrymen and overcome the tyranny of English rule is to fight, he becomes the ultimate patriot. The beliefs of soldiers are only as strong as the beliefs of their leader. The character of soldiers is only as strong as the character of their leader. Thus, Martin has to embody the beliefs and character of a true patriot in order to lead his men and by doing so, take a bite out of the English.

3. *Who/what keeps Martin from achieving what he wants?*

The British, of course, impede Martin's quest for revenge and are the reason his patriotism is necessary. Because many of the South Carolinians prefer not to fight and thus increase their odds of living, he wants for fighting men. Lack of supplies and rations is a constant pain. All the obstacles of warfare are also his to deal with. But those are the least of his problems. No force opposes him as vehemently as Tavington.

Tavington wants to kill Martin just as badly as Martin wants to kill him. He will go to any length necessary to destroy the Ghost and his men. This guy is pure evil, the compilation of every barbarous act and ungentlemanly deed of the worst British officers in *The Life of General Francis Marion*. He is given leave by Lord Cornwallis to use any means necessary to rid the British of this rebel nuisance. Tavington is the opposite of Martin, as any great villain should be. He is the result of an adaptation geared for a large audience and an equally large budget.

Before we go any further, please note that in no way whatsoever is Tavington a sympathetic villain. I bring this up because there's a movement in the movie industry right now that's based on the theory that all villains should be sympathetic so that the audience can identify with them. I'm not saying that sympathetic villains aren't a good thing (I've written my share of them), but there's always room for a good old-fashioned, mean mutha-shut-yo-mouth. The audience doesn't have to identify with the antagonist, they just have to hate him. The more you hate the bad guy, the happier you are when he gets his butt kicked in the end. And don't we all want to be happy?

4. *How in the end does Martin achieve what he wants in an unexpected, interesting, and unusual way?*

First, let's talk about the business of revenge. In film, when our hero kills the bad guy, we want it to be cool. If Martin had just shot Tavington, we'd have been let down. I'm sorry, but Tavington is so bad, he needs to go down in a really significant, heinous, and painful way. Here's a good outline of how these final conflicts generally work:

1. The good guy (let's call him Captain Phenomenal) finds the bad guy (we'll call him Deathtron 2000) and charges in headlong, full of fury, and thunder.
2. Captain Phenomenal gets in a couple good whacks, and it looks like he's really gonna pummel Deathtron 2000.
3. Uh-oh, Deathtron 2000 makes a surprising comeback and beats the bejesus out of Captain Phenomenal.
4. This looks like the end for Captain Phenomenal. Deathtron 2000 has him on the ropes, and he stops to say something menacing to really stick it to him before he ices him.
5. Deathtron 2000, you fool! You never should have given Captain Phenomenal that extra second to recoup. Whatever you said *really* pissed him off.
6. Captain Phenomenal gives Deathtron 2000 a sound drubbing and pauses to say something menacing, witty, and ofttimes a tad comical.
7. Two options at this point: One, Captain Phenomenal delivers the death blow. Two, Deathtron 2000 has one last move and then Captain Phenomenal delivers the death blow.

And there you have it. Please note, as a model, that this is a good sequence to try to avoid. At least try to make it fresh in such a way that it lacks predictability. One other important thing to remember about the way in which the hero dispatches the villain is that it has to be equal to or greater than (in terms of severity) the deeds the villain has committed to earn him such a death. That's why Tavington was impaled and received the ever-so-fashionable bayonet throat piercing. His body stays propped there until (we hope) the crows pick his flesh away. Works for me.

Now, how does this one man by the name of Benjamin Martin make a difference in the war? Not only do he and his men keep Cornwallis from moving north, but he single-handedly turns the tide of the last battle when he charges forth, Old Glory raised high, and rallies the troops for the final assault that will force a British retreat.

5. *What were they trying to say by ending the story this way?*

Patriotism is the one overriding idea that controls this story. What the story says in the end is that if you love your country and are truly a patriot, you will fight for it. War is necessary. If you don't fight for what you believe in, it will be taken from you. Freedom does not come without sacrifice. But in the end, the rewards of freedom outweigh the costs.

6. *How did they tell this story?*

Although the biography was written as a first-person narrative and could have been adapted in the same manner, the writer chose to tell it in the third person. It is straightforward, told chronologically, with no flashbacks or dream sequences, in a classic story structure.

7. *How do the main character and any supporting characters change over the course of the story?*

Benjamin Martin: Martin has changed from a man trying to forget his violent past, to a man who is forced to embrace his violent nature, and finally to a man who once again might have a chance for peace. He is a patriot, no doubt, but when he first ventures out onto the field of battle, his main concern is vengeance. When Gabriel dies, the fires of his vengeance are rekindled. Only in the final battle does he truly embrace a sense of true patriotism and to illustrate this, he raises that flag. Fighting for the cause, for the freedom of his country, is what finally allows him to exorcise the demons of his past. When he is motivated by the power of the cause instead of anger and vengeance, he finally truly succeeds. In doing so, he has also managed to work past the death of his wife and decide it'd be a pretty good idea to hook up with her sister. (I know this sounds kinda corny, but it works in the context of the film.)

Martin's men: The men who stand at the forefront of Martin's unit are changed by the war, some for the better, and others would have been changed for the better if they lived. The red-headed racist (who I believe may have been based on Scotch Macdonald) becomes best friends with the former slave who fought alongside him by the end. A preacher becomes a hell of a marksman, but is shot looking out for Gabriel. And they all become hardened, changed men. Most lost their families and loved ones. One cannot bear the cost and kills himself. All of his men are motivated to new heights of patriotism and heroism by Martin's actions and clearly grow into patriots themselves.

Gabriel Martin: When he enlists, I don't believe he has any real concept of what war is. The more experience he has with its terrors, the more he becomes like his father. When the costs of war come to include the death of his wife, he takes the path of rage and vengeance that ends up costing him his life.

The Big Seven: *The Patriot*

1. *Who is the main character?*
   Benjamin Martin.

2. *What does Benjamin want/need/desire?*

   He wants to be free, and to get revenge.

3. *Who/what keeps him from achieving what he wants?*

   Tavington, Cornwallis, and his own demons.

4. *How in the end does Benjamin achieve what he wants in an unexpected, interesting, and unusual way?*

   He kills Tavington with bullets made from his son's toy soldiers, and he also grabs the flag and leads the troops to victory.

5. *What are you trying to say by ending the story this way?*

   One patriot who believes deeply in freedom can change the world.

6. *How is the story told?*

   The story is told chronologically.

7. *How do your main character and any supporting characters change over the course of the story?*

   Please see the preceding pages.

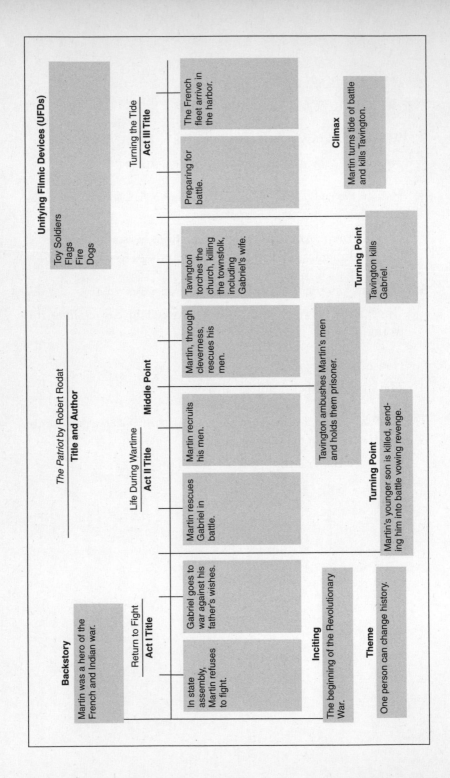

Unifying Filmic Devices (UFDs)

Toy Soldiers
Flags
Fire
Dogs

The Patriot by Robert Rodat
Title and Author

Turning the Tide
Act III Title

The French fleet arrive in the harbor.

Preparing for battle.

Climax

Martin turns tide of battle and kills Tavington.

Life During Wartime
Act II Title   **Middle Point**

Martin rescues Gabriel in battle.

Martin recruits his men.

Martin, through cleverness, rescues his men.

Tavington torches the church, killing the townsfolk, including Gabriel's wife.

Tavington ambushes Martin's men and holds them prisoner.

Turning Point

Tavington kills Gabriel.

Turning Point

Martin's younger son is killed, sending him into battle vowing revenge.

Backstory

Martin was a hero of the French and Indian war.

Return to Fight
Act I Title

In state assembly, Martin refuses to fight.

Gabriel goes to war against his father's wishes.

Inciting

The beginning of the Revolutionary War.

Theme

One person can change history.

8

Reinterpreting and Reinventing the Storytelling Wheel

Case Study: *O Brother, Where Art Thou?*

When the Coen brothers adapted Homer's *The Odyssey* into their parody *O Brother, Where Art Thou?*, what they were actually adapting was really an adaptation of an earlier work. Homer's *The Odyssey* is really a compilation of many different stories that he wove all together into his own adaptation that we call *The Odyssey*.

You probably read it in college, high school, or, if you were a wunderkind, junior high school. There have been both film and television miniseries adaptations of *The Odyssey* produced over the years. These have all been standard, traditional, straightforward adaptations of the work. Obviously, the Coen boys didn't yearn to do the same and merely transcribe *The Odyssey* into another run-of-the-mill literary classic on film. What they did is use Homer's work as a starting point. And if you can't tell, the film *O Brother* opens with an onscreen credit that states that this film is based on Homer's classic work. Some might say that it would have been more appropriate to say that *O Brother* is really inspired by *The Odyssey* rather than based on it. But hey, let's not get into a debate on semantics. Either way, we are talking about a freewheeling Homeric adaptation set in the American South during the 1930s.

There is a great deal of precedent for this kind of adaptation. Ironically, modern popular novels like *Harry Potter* are actually less open to filmic reinterpretation than traditional literary classics. In general, I believe this stems from the fact that the classics have all already been adapted in traditional ways and we yearn to see their stories told differently, while texts like *Harry Potter* have yet to be adapted to the screen.

This concept of reinterpreting classic texts as one adapts them is far from new. Shakespeare reinterpreted and adapted many historical events and turned them into plays. In keeping with this trend, his play *Romeo and Juliet* has been adapted to numerous settings and time periods, including its most famous adaptation, *West Side Story*, which was set in what was then, modern-day New York City. The Coen brothers have essentially done a similar thing with Homer's classic. They have taken a landmark work and set it in a different time with different characters and a different language. Yet it's far from a cut-and-paste job. A new story has been created, and in it we can see the inspiration of *The Odyssey*.

Let's start at the beginning of the story of *O Brother, Where Art Thou?* and explore the choices that the Coen brothers made in their adaptation. Everett (George Clooney) is Odysseus. Pete (John Turturro) and Delmar (Tim Blake Nelson) are his companions and serve as stand-ins for Homeric characters. As the story begins, Everett, Pete, and Delmar have escaped from a chain gang, and a blind seer with no name comes down the railroad tracks on one of those hand-pump cart things. He tells these adventurers what lies ahead, functioning in the story in a similar manner to a certain blind prophet in *The Odyssey* who went by the name of Teiresias, the most gifted of all the prophets. Odysseus sees him in Hades, and the soothsayer tells him of the great troubles ahead. He tells him it will be a long time before he reaches home, and when he does, he will be "in an evil plight upon a foreign ship, with all your comrades dead."

Teiresias also warns Odysseus that none of his men are to eat the cattle of Hyperion, lest a grave fate befall them all (this prophecy manifests itself more directly in *O Brother*). In the film, the seer's prediction of the men seeing a cow on the roof of a cotton shed isn't quite as foreboding, but it serves its purpose. He also tells Everett and the boys that they will find treasure, though it is not the treasure they seek. And he informs them that their journey will be difficult and fraught with peril, just as Odysseus's was.

There's another parallel here as well. Odysseus's tale begins on an island where he's been held prisoner by the witch Calypso for several years. Everett begins his quest by escaping from a chain gang. It's not exactly being held captive by a sultry witch, but he has been imprisoned and now he is free. Odysseus is going back to his family. Though we don't know it yet, Everett is going back to his wife and children as well.

We're just scratching the surface of the manifestations of Homer's story found in the Coen brothers' adaptation, and we'll continue to look at them more closely. But for now, let's think about how one goes about this kind of adaptation. When you're dealing with one of the most widely read works in the Western world and you attempt to do a serious, direct adaptation, surely the scrutiny will be severe. If you don't want to open up that Pandora's box but prefer to flex your creative muscles in a different way, consider the route the Coen brothers took.

Consider a parody adaptation. No, this doesn't mean the Cyclops should wear a pink party dress and have an intimate relationship with his sheep, although that might seem funny to some people. It means creating a different story that mirrors the original. But the mirrors you must employ are the kind you'd find in a carnival funhouse. If the film hadn't told you it was based on *The Odyssey*, would you have known? Maybe, maybe not. The truth is that the screenplay must stand on its own, but once you do know, there's a great deal of fun in searching for the similarities.

So, then, let's explore the specific steps that one might use in attempting to construct a parody adaptation. Step one, extract the characters you're going to use from the original text. Find a way to present them in an original and interesting way. Step two, extract the events you want to use from the original work. Weave them into your story so the similarities can be seen but are not too on the nose. Step three, inject levity. Sounds easy, but as with most things, it's easier said than done.

It's difficult to make these kinds of decisions in any adaptation. What it really comes down to is developing your story. You've got more latitude here than you have with most other adaptations. When it comes to the alleged levity injection, you must walk the line between being clever yet silly, and attempting to be clever but ending up being past the left field side of stupidity.

This is an adaptation that really requires a storyteller's skills. Not that other adaptations don't, but here (perhaps more than with other more traditional types of adaptations), the adaptor is forced to create and massage the elements of the original into a new story altogether. Sure, it's still the story of a man trying to get home to his family, but beyond that, it's a whole new ball game. So now let's take some time to analyze what the Coen boys have done with their new story, *O Brother, Where Art Thou?*

1. *Who is the main character?*

    Ulysses Everett McGill—ah, what a name! Everett's name has the beautiful ring of irony, in that he is a low-down scoundrel, yet his name sounds very highfalutin'. It's the same dichotomy you'd get by serving hog jowls and caviar. The name is a joke in and of itself. Odysseus's name, however, actually means something. Though scholars still debate its meaning to this day, it's generally agreed that it means "man of pain," or "man of trouble," which closely parallels the Soggy Bottom Boys' hit "Man of Constant Sorrow." Everett, like Odysseus, is never at a loss for words, though we get the feeling that Everett might not understand half of what he's saying. At his core, he wants the same things Odysseus wanted.

2. *What does Everett want/need/desire?*

    As the movie opens, Everett wants to be free. He's been on the chain gang for quite some time. This is the opening scene and the start of his journey. Once he's escaped, the next order of business is to remain free. The audience and his compadres are fooled into thinking that Everett is on a quest to find a treasure he's buried, but as it turns out, he's on the way home to his family (which some might also label a treasure). Just like Odysseus, he wants to rid his wife of her suitors. (Everett's wife only has one suitor, while in *The Odyssey* there were a whole host of suitors hanging out at Odysseus's place. They ate all his food, drank his wine, and otherwise drained his resources.) As the *paterfamilias*, Everett wants his family back, and he believes he deserves them back, by God!

3. *Who/what keeps Everett from achieving what he wants?*

This is where the creativity of the Coens really shines. The bulk of *The Odyssey* is the telling of Odysseus's journey, his trials and tribulations. The Coens had the task of massaging these trials and tribulations into their time and locale. I'll list a few of the major antagonists here, and we'll see from whence they were derived later in this chapter. The lead characters—Everett, Delmar, and Pete—argue among themselves, but Everett always manages to keep the peace, despite the forces aligned against them. He's a born leader, just like Odysseus, but he has his work cut out for him. Nature, man, and the gods conspire in one way or another to destroy them. The law pursues them relentlessly, one-eyed Big Dan Teque beats and robs them, the Sirens turn one of them (Pete) into a frog (well, not really, but it seems true at the time) and then over to the authorities. In addition, the place where their money is hidden will be flooded soon (a time constraint), a suitor (Vernon T. Waldrip) has claimed Everett's wife as his own, and even their relatives turn them in for a bounty.

What makes this story different from most is the lack of one central villain, an evil wellspring from which all of the antagonism flows. You could argue that it's the satanic, sunglassed leader of the posse pursuing them, but he is simply another force among many that seek to destroy our hero. This is an odyssey, and along the way, Everett encounters a plethora of problems. In Homer's work, Poseidon was behind the majority of Odysseus's troubles, but we don't have that central figure in *O Brother*. At least, we don't have that active a central or primary antagonist. There are some suspects, but we'll get to that later.

4. *How in the end does Everett succeed in an original/interesting/ unusual way?*

Everett and the Soggy Bottom Boys eventually win their freedom through song. Everett, of course, gets his wife back, but she gives him one final task, to find her ring and bring it back to her. When Everett and the boys go to get the ring, the satanic head of the posse is there waiting for them. There is a point at which man can do no more, and divine intervention is needed. In other words, here comes the deus ex machina. Odysseus was assisted many times by the gods of old, most notably by Athena, who favored him. Just when things seem to be over for the Soggy Bottom Boys, a great flood saves them. There are bits of information about the forthcoming flooding of the Mississippi Valley planted throughout the film, so in some ways when this does occur, this does not seem like a completely divine event, but rather a natural and organic part of the story. However, to complicate things even further, the Coens have the flood come as a direct result of the prayers of our hero, Everett, who up to this point has been everything but a religious man.

5. *What are they trying to say by ending the story this way?*

Throughout the story, Everett finds a way to explain everything with logic. He's utterly amused by Pete and Delmar being "saved." Then he finds out that Tommy Johnson sold his soul to the devil. By this time, he's the only one who remains "unaffiliated." When the valley is flooded and he sees the cow atop the cotton shed, he's forced to reconsider his views of life. Maybe there is a God, and maybe he listens. Since the blind old man predicted it all, he's also forced to consider fate. But hey, this is a parody, so when Everett survives the flood, he has the wrong ring. Although maybe it was just fate or God's hand that led him to the wrong wedding ring . . .

6. *How did they tell this story?*

This is a tale told in the third person, without a narrator. In many ways, *O Brother* is quite close to being a musical. In a traditional musical, the characters break into song when they've got something important to say. In this story, the music comes about as a result of our characters' circumstances. It's used to accentuate and punctuate the tone of each scene. And it is music that eventually wins the Soggy Bottom Boys their freedom.

Music plays an entirely different role in the life of Tommy Johnson. Here's where the Coens have mixed in a famous fable in Southern mythology. According to this legend, the father of the blues, Robert Johnson, knelt at midnight at a crossroads in Clarksdale, Mississippi, and the devil appeared to him. They struck a deal whereby Johnson sold his soul to the devil and in exchange was given the gift of being the world's greatest blues guitarist. This explained Johnson's phenomenal blues mastery at such a young age. However, the devil was an impatient man, and Robert Johnson died in 1938 at the age of only twenty-seven. Tommy Johnson's story is obviously based on this legend, and it is interesting to note that the boys first meet him at a crossroads, at which point he tells them of striking a deal at midnight with the devil.

7. *How do the main character and any other characters change over the course of the story?*

Everett is forced to consider the possibility of fate and God. Pete, Delmar, and Everett have all managed to make an honest living by the end of the film. Mrs. McGill is no longer telling her children that their father is dead, and she's accepted him as a bona fide suitor. Governor Pappy O'Daniel has risen from the bottom of the polls to the top again, thanks to the Soggy Bottom Boys. Homer Stokes, who was previously the friend of the little man, is revealed as the KKK-leading, hypocritical SOB that he really is.

There are no real tremendous character arcs in this story because there were no real tremendous arcs in characters in *The Odyssey*. Yes, Telemachus changes from a boy to a man, and learns what it is to be a man. Other characters exhibit minor changes in attitude, but not our main character, Odysseus. His worldview has not radically changed as a result of his tribulations. To a certain degree, he overcomes his hubris, and he definitely pays for being excessively prideful, but in the same way that

Everett finds God at the climax of the movie, even at the end of the book, you never really believe that Odysseus is a changed man. Odysseus did, however, achieve his goal and was reunited with his family. Now he can live happily ever after. Once he slaughters the suitors who have besieged his home, of course.

There's our outline of this story via the Big Seven. The real task of parody adaptation is massaging elements from the original story into a new tale. As a whole, examining how the Coen brothers did it with this classic Homeric tale demonstrates the tremendous leeway and fun a creative adaptor can have with a text.

Think about a classic tale that might work being reimagined in another locale or era. I took Shakespeare's *King Lear*, made it into a modern comedy of three daughters who take over their father's company, and called it *King Levine*. The sky's the limit when you have the basic structure and themes of a great tale. You can set it anywhere, and it should always work. And if you go in the direction of a parody for your adaptation, you are forced to be imaginative while not being too on the nose. You don't have to perfectly reflect every instance of the original work. Remember, it's *based* on the original material, and as you already know by now, you owe nothing to the original work.

If there's ever been a story about an engaging character overcoming tremendous obstacles to reach a desirable goal, it's *The Odyssey*. Keep that phrase in mind as you continue to write. Use it as a rudder to steer your course of adaptation. You can stray far from the original material, but you can't stray far from that guiding principle.

It's important that you make your story solid. Such is the case with any story, but especially with an adaptation. The fact is, many people may not even know your story is an adaptation. You've probably seen dozens of films based on other stories and not even realized they were adaptations. All you thought about was whether the story worked on its own or not. The bottom line is that you can't rely on the source material to give your story substance. Sure, it helps if the source material story is good, but as with any written form, it is your skills as a storyteller that will set you apart from the pack.

The Big Seven: *O Brother, Where Art Thou?*

1. *Who is the main character?*

   Everett Ulysses McGill is our main character.

2. *What does Everett want/need/desire?*

   He wants to get home to his wife and children. On an emotional level, he wants to be loved by his wife and family and respected by his friends. He also wants to deny that there is a God, but he changes his tune as the story progresses.

3. *Who/what keeps Everett from achieving what he wants?*

   The law, nature, God, Satan, and his wife.

4. *How in the end does Everett succeed in an original/interesting/ unusual way?*

   Everett and the Soggy Bottom Boys win over the governor and Mrs. McGill. In addition, in the very end, his faith allows him to overcome Satan and survive the big flood.

5. *What are they trying to say by ending the story this way?*

   Try as they might, men cannot fight fate/God's will.

6. *How did they tell this story?*

   In the third person, no flashbacks, no voice-over, music used to organically accentuate themes, scenes, and motifs.

7. *How do the main character and any other characters change over the course of the story?*

   Everett is forced to consider the ideas of fate and faith. Pete, Delmar, and Everett are all making an honest living.

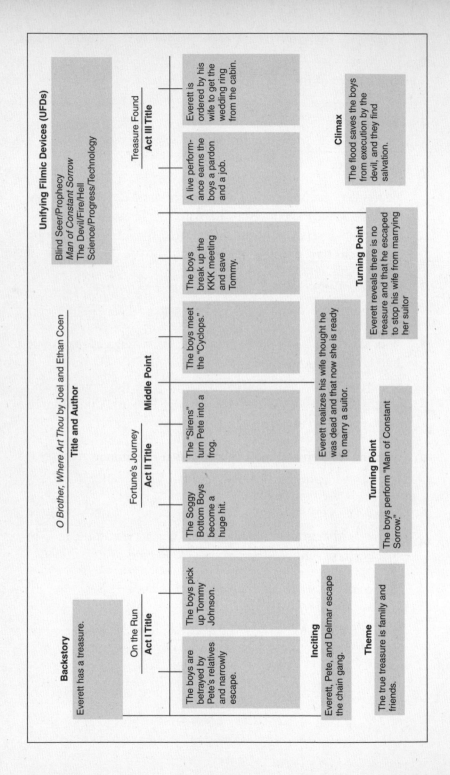

Unifying Filmic Devices (UFDs)

Blind Seer/Prophecy
Man of Constant Sorrow
The Devil/Fire/Hell
Science/Progress/Technology

Title and Author

O Brother, Where Art Thou by Joel and Ethan Coen

Backstory

Everett has a treasure.

On the Run
Act I Title

Fortune's Journey
Act II Title

Treasure Found
Act III Title

The boys are betrayed by Pete's relatives and narrowly escape.

The boys pick up Tommy Johnson.

The Soggy Bottom Boys become a huge hit.

The "Sirens" turn Pete into a frog.

Middle Point

The boys meet the "Cyclops."

The boys break up the KKK meeting and save Tommy.

A live performance earns the boys a pardon and a job.

Everett is ordered by his wife to get the wedding ring from the cabin.

Inciting

Everett, Pete, and Delmar escape the chain gang.

Everett realizes his wife thought he was dead and that now she is ready to marry a suitor.

Everett reveals there is no treasure and that he escaped to stop his wife from marrying her suitor

Climax

The flood saves the boys from execution by the devil, and they find salvation.

Turning Point

The boys perform "Man of Constant Sorrow."

Turning Point

Theme

The true treasure is family and friends.

9

I Know It Really Happened That Way, But . . .

Case Study: *Madison*

Anything can spark a writer's imagination. There are thousands of stories in newspapers and magazines every day that might lend themselves to being adapted into a screenplay. How do you pick the right one? How do you know which newspaper column or magazine article is really the one that's going to provide the seed material for that commercially viable script? There's really only one way to know for sure: The story has to fascinate you, interest you, engage you.

If you're not getting paid to write the screenplay, the only thing that is going to keep you motivated through the arduous process is your love and passion for the story. If the story moves you—really moves you—then you must tell it, and in the telling of it, you may also move the world. Adapt a story because you want to tell it, because you want other people to know the tale as you know it. Make an investment in the material. You might also need to invest some money as well. But most importantly, there must be an investment of your talents and your time; be sure to invest enough of both to do the story justice.

This is exactly what brothers Scott and William Bindley did. They spent fourteen years working on a true-life story and bringing it to the big screen. The story that moved them so deeply was a real underdog story, a true American heroic tale that was called *Madison*.

Madison is a tale based on the true story of the *Miss Madison*, the only community-owned boat on the hydroplane power boat racing circuit. In 1971, a crew of volunteers and driver Jim McCormick beat all the odds to win the APBA (American Power Boat Association) Gold Cup on the Ohio River in front of a hometown crowd in Madison, Indiana. There are no famous books about this event. There is not a lot of information to be found on it. However, there is a quite comprehensive article written about it by Fred Farley, a writer who's covered the APBA unlimited circuit for forty years. This article first appeared in the 1984 *Madison Regatta Program* magazine.

An aspiring screenwriter can learn a great deal by looking at the article and my interview of screenwriter Scott Bindley and observing what choices were made in transforming this true-life tale into a classically structured three-act Hollywood screenplay that really works.

So now let's read a reprint of a beautifully written article by Fred Farley called "Miss Madison, the Gold Cup Champion," which tells the basic events of the story captured in the film Madison. (Please note that this article has been edited to fit into this chapter, and it is reprinted with the permission of its author.) And then, after reading the article, please peruse my interview of screenwriter Scott Bindley before moving on to my analysis. Enjoy.

Miss Madison, the Gold Cup Champion

by Fred Farley

No one who attended the fabulous 1971 APBA Gold Cup Regatta in Madison, Indiana, will ever forget it. That was when *Miss Madison*, the world's only community-owned and sponsored Unlimited hydroplane, confounded the oddsmakers, winning the race of races before the hometown crowd. The *Miss Madison*'s richly sentimental triumph on that memorable July 4 was an historic one on several counts. Not since the 1965 Dixie Cup at Guntersville, Alabama, had the sun-bleached Miss M scored a victory. It was pilot Jim McCormick's first win ever in the Unlimited Class. The *Miss Madison* was built in 1959 and first entered competition in

1960, thereby making her the only Unlimited hydroplane ever to win a Gold Cup eleven years after its competitive debut. Not since mandatory qualifications began in 1949 had a Gold Cup winner placed lower than fourth on the qualifying speed ladder. (Miss M was seventh.)

The 1971 event also marked the first and only time that a community-owned boat has ever won the Gold Cup. Not since 1966 had the American Power Boat Association's Crown Jewel been won by a boat with Allison—rather than Rolls-Royce—aircraft power. The *Miss Madison* of 1971 also represented the end of an era. (She was the last Unlimited hydroplane with the old-style rear cockpit/forward engine/shovel-nosed bow configuration to ever achieve victory.) The hull that became the Gold Cup–winning Miss M was designed and built by Les Staudacher of Kawkawlin, Michigan. Staudacher had previously constructed such successful contenders as *Miss Pepsi, Gale V, Tempo VIII, Miss Thriftway,* and *Hawaii Kai III*. The future *Miss Madison* measured 30 feet in length with a 12-foot beam. Made of marine plywood and aluminum, she tipped the scales at close to 7000 lb. in racing trim.

Jim McCormick of Owensboro, Kentucky, made his Unlimited Class debut as driver of the community-owned entry in 1966, replacing Buddy Byers who had signed on to drive Bill Harrah's *Tahoe Miss*. In 1969, the now-experienced Jim McCormick returned to the cockpit. But even with the change in drivers, the boat's performance did not improve. A third at the hometown Madison Regatta was the team's highest finish. Indeed, the glory days of 1964–65 seemed light years away.

Miss Madison almost missed the 1970 campaign entirely on account of being involved in a highway accident in Georgia while en route to the first race of the season in Tampa, Florida. Pulled off the circuit, the stricken craft underwent repairs by original builder Les Staudacher. In retrospect, the mishap was probably a blessing. Staudacher used the occasion to go through the entire hull and fix several things in addition to the highway accident damage that might otherwise have gone unnoticed.

At year's end, *Miss Madison* was running the best of her long career and giving the better-than-average performance that was expected of her. She could make the front runners work for it and could run with them on occasion. But the general consensus at the outset of 1971 was that only a newer hull and more power would put the U-6 team in the winner's circle. Nevertheless, the *Miss Madison* organization decided to stay with their eleven—going on twelve—year old craft for one more season.

The Thunderboat trail now led to Madison, Indiana, which was steeped in a competitive tradition that dated back to 1911. As things developed, the city's 60th boat racing anniversary story would have amazed a fiction writer. No publisher would have accepted a make-believe script on the race.

For the first time since 1951, the Indiana Governor's Cup shared the spotlight with the APBA Gold Cup, power boating's Crown Jewel, which had never before been run in so small a town as Madison. Due to a technicality and a misunderstanding, the $30,000 bid for the race by the sponsoring Madison Regatta, Inc., was the only one submitted in time to the Gold Cup Contest Board.

For ten years, the volunteer *Miss Madison* mechanical crew had tried to win the hometown race without success. They faced an uphill fight in 1971, and they knew it. In the first four races of the season, *Miss Budweiser* and *Atlas Van Lines I* had both scored two solid victories apiece. *Atlas Van Lines II*, a five-race winner in 1969–70, was likewise a formidable contender. (Having been her team's number one entry during the three previous years, the *II*'s performance had suffered little in her secondary role with Terry Sterett in the cockpit.)

Several days before the race, Jim McCormick placed a

crucial telephone call to Reno, Nevada. He requested and obtained the services of two of the finest Allison engine specialists in the sport—Harry Volpi and Everett Adams of the defunct Harrah's Club racing team—who flew to Madison and worked in the pits alongside U-6 regulars Tony Steinhardt, Bob Humphrey, Dave Stewart, Keith Hand, and Russ Willey. Volpi and Adams are credited with perfecting the *Miss Madison's* water-alcohol injection system.

Race day, July 4, 1971, dawned bright and warm with ten qualified boats prepared to do competitive battle. A crowd of 110,000 fans literally choked the small Midwestern town of 13,000. The river conditions were good, but Miss M was down to her last engine, having blown the other in trials. This put the U-6 people at a distinct disadvantage, because, at that time, the Gold Cup Race consisted of four 15-mile heats instead of the usual three.

The race was less than thirty seconds old when *Hallmark Homes* disintegrated in a geyser of spray and sank in the first turn of Heat 1-A, after encountering the roostertail of *Atlas Van Lines I*. Hallmark pilot Leif Borgersen escaped injury, but his boat was totaled.

Miss Madison was drawn into Heat 1-B along with *Towne Club*, *Miss Timex*, *The Smoother Mover*, and *Atlas Van Lines II*. During the warm-up period, *Smoother Mover* joined *Hallmark Homes* at the bottom of the river when her supercharger blew and punched a hole in the *Mover's* underside.

Miss M had the lead at the end of lap one but was then passed by *Atlas II*. On lap three, the Fred Alter-chauffeured *Towne Club* began to challenge *Miss Madison* for second place. McCormick and Alter see-sawed back and forth for several laps and brought the crowd to its feet. Miss M managed to outrun the *Towne Club* and hang on for second place points behind the front-running *Atlas II*.

For the second round of preliminaries, *Miss Madison*

matched skills with *Miss Budweiser*, *Notre Dame* and *Atlas I* in Heat 2-B. Bill Muncey reached the first turn first with *Atlas I*, followed by *Miss M*, *Budweiser* and *Notre Dame* who were both watered down by Muncey's roostertail, causing both to go dead in the water. *Atlas I* widened its lead over the field down the first backstretch and in the ensuing laps, while *Miss Madison* settled into a safe second. *Miss Budweiser* immediately restarted to follow Miss M around the course in third place. *Notre Dame* also managed to restart but only after being lapped by the field.

At the end of 15 miles, Muncey and *Atlas I* received the green flag instead of the checkered flag, indicating a one lap penalty for a foul against *Miss Budweiser* and *Notre Dame* in the first turn for violation of the overlap rule. This moved *Miss Madison* from second to first position in the corrected order of finish. *Miss Budweiser* was given second place, and *Atlas I* wound up officially in third after running seven laps before *Notre Dame* could finish six. After another random draw, Miss M found herself in Heat 3-B along with *Atlas II*, *Notre Dame*, and *Pride of Pay 'n Pak*.

As Bill Muncey was preparing to drive *Atlas I* before Heat 3-A, he received word that Referee Bill Newton had put him on probation for the next three races of the season. The probation had resulted not only from the foul against the field in Heat 2-B but also from the cumulative effect of similar infractions by Muncey in 1970 at Seattle and San Diego. The consequence of the probation was that any further violations by Muncey would result in an indefinite suspension from racing.

Unperturbed, Muncey made a good start in Heat 3-A and was chasing Dean Chenoweth and *Miss Budweiser* down the first backstretch when *Atlas I* sheared off her right sponson and started taking on water. Bill frantically tried to steer his wounded craft toward the bank on the Kentucky side of the river but was unable to do so. *Atlas Van Lines I* rolled over on its side about 100 feet from shore and slipped beneath the surface, forcing Muncey to abandon ship. Now, three boats rested at the bottom of the Ohio.

Terry Sterett and *Atlas II* entered the first turn of Heat 3-B in the lead and stayed there, but *Miss Madison* kept nipping at their heels. *Pride of Pay 'n Pak*, running in third, tried to overtake Miss M, but the U-6 pulled away to maintain second position. On the last lap, *Miss Madison* came on hard to finish only two seconds behind *Atlas II* and four seconds ahead of *Pay 'n Pak*.

After three grueling sets of elimination heats, the five qualifiers for the final go-around comprised *Atlas II* with 1100 accumulated points, *Miss Madison* with 1000 points, *Pride of Pay 'n Pak* with 869, *Towne Club* with 750, and *Miss Budweiser* with 700.

As the sun started to set on that historic July 4, the race for the Gold Cup and the Governor's Cup boiled down to *Atlas Van Lines II* and *Miss Madison*. Miss M had to make up a deficit of 100 points in order to win the championship. To do this, the U-6 would have to finish first in the final 15-mile moment of truth. This appeared rather unlikely since the combination of Terry Sterett and *Atlas II* had bested the team of Jim McCormick and *Miss Madison* in each of their four previous match-ups that season, twice on the Ohio River and twice the previous weekend on the Detroit River.

As the field took to the water for the last time, some of the hometown fans hung on to the hope that perhaps *Atlas II* would fail to start and thereby allow the local favorite to win the big race by default. But that was not to be. As McCormick wheeled Miss M out onto the 2½-mile course, there was Sterett, starting up and pulling out of the pit area right behind him. Thus, as the final minutes and seconds ticked away, the die was cast. If McCormick hoped to achieve his first career victory on this day, he would have to earn it—the hard way.

Meanwhile, the ABC "Wide World of Sports" television crew members, who were there taping the race for a delayed national broadcast, decided among themselves that Terry Sterett was a shoo-in for the title. Accordingly, they set up their camera equipment in the *Atlas II*'s pit area in anticipation of interviewing the victorious Sterett when he returned to the dock.

All five finalists were on the course and running. Moments before the one-minute gun, Miss Madison was observed cruising down the front straightaway in front of the pit area. Then, abruptly, McCormick altered course, making a hard left turn into the infield. He sped across course, making a bee-line for the entrance buoy of the upper corner. His strategy was obvious. McCormick wanted the inside lane to force the other boats to run a wider—and longer—course.

As the field charged underneath the Milton/Madison Bridge, four of the five boats were closely bunched with Fred Alter's *Towne Club* on the extreme outside, skirting the shoreline. *Miss Madison* had lane one; *Atlas Van Lines II* had lane two and was slightly in the lead when the starting gun fired.

Sprinting toward the first turn, *Pride of Pay 'n Pak* spun out. *Atlas II* made it into and out of the turn in front with *Miss Madison* close behind on the inside. As the field entered the first backstretch, the order was *Atlas, Madison, Budweiser, Pay 'n Pak,* and *Towne Club.*

Then McCormick made his move. After having run a steady conservative race all day long, "Gentleman Jim" slammed the accelerator to the floor. The boat took off like a shot and thundered past Terry Sterett as if his rival had been tied to the dock.

The partisan crowd screamed in unison, "GO! GO! GO!" Even hardened veterans of racing were dumbfounded. An aging, under-powered, under-financed museum piece was leading the race and leaving the rest of the field to wallow in its wake.

McCormick whipped Miss M around the upper turn expertly and sped under the bridge and back down the river to the start/finish line. It was one down and five laps to go. The *Atlas*, the *Budweiser*, and the *Pay 'n Pak* were closely bunched at this point as they followed *Miss Madison* around the buoys.

The crowd was going absolutely wild. In lap two, McCormick increased his lead. And, in lap three, he extended his advantage even more. It dawned on the "Wide World of Sports" crew that an upset was in the making. Frantically, the ABC-TV technicians scrambled out of the *Atlas* pit area and hustled their camera gear over to the *Miss Madison*'s pits.

Out on the race course, Sterett had shaken free of *Budweiser* and *Pay 'n Pak* and was going all out after Miss M. He was fast on the straightaways, but not as fast as McCormick. The *Atlas* cornered well, but not as well as the U-6.

Miss Madison was running flawlessly, her 26-year-old Allison engine not missing a beat. Jim McCormick was driving the race of his life. Together, the boat and driver made an inspired combination. Bonnie McCormick, Jim's wife, who had averted her eyes during the first few laps, was now concentrating fully on the action, cheering her husband on at the top of her lungs.

Miss M received the green flag, indicating one more lap to the checkered flag and victory. By now, the community-owned craft had a decisive lead. Sterett was beaten, and he knew it. The *Atlas* pilot could only hope against hope that a mechanical problem or a driving error would slow the Miss M down.

But that didn't happen. McCormick made one last perfect turn. The Miss M's roostertail kicked skyward. The boat streaked under the bridge, past Bennett's dock, and over the finish line, adding a new chapter to American sports legend, as pandemonium broke loose on the shore.

Firebells rang, automobile horns sounded, and the spectators went out of their minds with delight. Everybody, it seemed, was a U-6 fan and, whether they lived there or not, a Madisonian. Even members of rival teams were applauding the outcome of this modern day Horatio Alger story.

Miss Madison had beaten *Atlas Van Lines II* by 16.3 seconds in the Final Heat and was 4.2 seconds swifter for the overall 60 miles. McCormick and Sterett had tied with 1400 points a piece in the four heats of racing. According to Unlimited Class rules, a point tie is broken by the order of finish in the last heat of the day. So, the U-6 won all the marbles. These included an engraved plate that would say *Miss Madison,* to be added to the rows of gleaming testimonials to the conquests of Gar Wood, George Reis, Danny Foster, Stan Sayres, Bill Muncey, and others.

It was the biggest day in the history of Madison, Indiana. It was Unlimited hydroplane racing at its best. It was a victory for the amateur, for the common man, a triumph that everyone could claim as his own. And not since the Slo-mo-shun days in Seattle during the 1950s had such an outpouring of civic emotion occurred at a Gold Cup Race with people celebrating in the streets until 10 o'clock that night.

Deliriously happy *Miss Madison* crew-members carried pilot McCormick on their shoulders to the Judges' Stand. Veteran boat racer George N. Davis, a mentor of McCormick's during Jim's 280 Class career, wept unashamedly at this, his protege's, moment of triumph.

After receiving the Gold Cup from 1946 winner Guy Lombardo and the Governor's Cup from Indiana Governor Edgar Whitcomb, a tired but happy McCormick explained his race strategy to the assembled legion of awe-struck media representatives. "We planned to take it easy in the early heats, and then let it all hang out in the finals."

McCormick was the first to give credit where credit was due. He quickly acknowledged that without the mechanical prowess of his volunteer pit crew, victory would have been impossible. "These guys have been working their hearts out getting ready for this. They deserve all the credit."

The *Miss Madison* crew received the Mark A. Lytle

Sportsmanship Trophy at the Gold Cup Awards Banquet, where tribute was also paid to the two former Harrah's Club team members—Volpi and Adams—for their invaluable help in winning "the big one."

"Gentleman Jim" McCormick, who had achieved his "Impossible Dream," was the hero of the day, and he gratefully acknowledged the enthusiasm of the crowd. For several hours after the trophy presentation, McCormick, still in his driving suit, remained at the Judges' Stand, signing his name for one and all. "Let the people come," he said. "I'll sign autographs as long as I can write." It was the perfect ending to a perfect day.

As the spectators and participants drifted back to their own lives, one thought was uppermost in the minds of many: "Was it all a dream, or did today really happen?"

(NOTE: The author of this article is indebted to David Greene and Philip Haldeman, both of the APBA Unlimited Historical Committee, for their editorial assistance.)

Writer Scott Bindley was gracious enough to agree to talk with me about the process he went through in adapting the incredible true-life story of hydroplane boat racing on the Ohio River in Madison, Indiana, the *Miss Madison* and Jim McCormick and his family. Please note that Bindley spent many days interviewing people and reading accounts of the events surrounding the *Miss Madison's* Gold Cup Victory. Even if you have an incredible imagination, often there is no substitute for doing your homework as a writer. Read everything you can on the subject. Interview anyone who will talk with you. Become an expert on the subject area, and that expertise will shine through in the specifics of your storytelling.

Scott Bindley is solely credited as a screenwriter on 1991's *Miracle Beach*, as well as 1995's *Johnny & Clyde*. He has sold nine screenplays and written dozens of magazine features for *Men's Journal*, *Men's Health*, *Playboy*, *Mademoiselle*, *Penthouse*, and many others. He lives in Indianapolis, Indiana, with his wife, Polly.

An Interview with Scott Bindley

Q: *How did you first hear about the story?*

A: I first heard about the story when I was a senior at Northwestern University in 1988. My brother, William Bindley, was in Indianapolis, prepping a Disney Channel film he was about to direct, when he heard of the Madison story through a mutual friend who had been to Madison covering an unrelated story for the *Indianapolis Star* newspaper. It turns out the 1971 Gold Cup story was the biggest thing to ever happen in Madison. My brother asked if I would be interested in writing the screenplay with him, and I finagled the project into a college credit at school.

We spent a day in Madison and met with the folks involved in the true story and took some initial notes. Later, I returned with my tape recorder and spent a weekend discussing the events of 1971 with several of the crew members of the *Miss Madison* team. I had only prepared a couple of questions, but had a hunch that it would take very little to get these guys going once they started to reminisce. I sat at a card table in the basement of the 1971 *Miss Madison* crew chief and one of the team mechanics, popped open a few beers, and started looking through old scrapbooks of photos and newspaper clippings. I turned on my tape recorder and four hours later had plenty to get started with. It was one of the most special memories of my writing career. It seemed that every photo led to a story about overcoming some kind of obstacle the crew faced.

Several times, these two men (in their early fifties) found themselves wiping away tears as they came upon photos of friends and competitors who had died. Hydroplane racing was an extremely dangerous sport, particularly during the 1960s and 1970s. There was an old saying at the time—"What this sport needs more than anything are some retired champions." It seemed that all of the best drivers of that era were killed in accidents, and very few walked away from the sport unscathed. (I have always loved the power of that line, and we had it in the screenplay in several places, but it did not make the final cut.) Anyway, that is how the project got started, and I think we wrote about half of the first draft while I was in school, and I continued working on it after graduation. I did lots of research and the best article I could find on the Gold Cup was one written by Fred Farley.

Q: *How did you go about optioning the rights?*

A: We secured the rights of the driver in the story, who became our main character. We had a very simple option contract drawn up and it was signed by Jim McCormick, his wife, Bonnie, and their son Mike, who became the vehicles from which we told the story. For many years, the script was entitled *Roostertail*, which is the name given to the giant water sprayed out behind the powerful racing boats. We briefly called it *American Pie* as this was an all-American success story, and took place the summer the Don McLean song came out (but we all know where that title went). We settled on *Madison* as a temporary title, with the intention of changing it later (but we never came up with anything better and people seemed to like it). Every year or so, my brother called me and asked me to send him $1,000 or so to cover my half of the option extension, which we renewed many times before the project finally got off the ground. For a long time, I wondered if we were simply throwing this money away—it's one thing not to sell something, but to pay out of my own pocket at the same time was particularly difficult.

Q: *How did you then go about transferring the story into a screenplay, and please talk about the specifics of what you had to leave out and add?*

A: I felt very strongly about staying close to the absolute truth on the first draft of the screenplay. I felt we owed it to the people who lived this story to research it properly and see how well it stood on its own before we started tinkering. I spent hours tape recording phone conversations with everyone involved in the story—all of the living crew members, their wives, the mayor of

Madison, and the real Harry Volpi, who is played in the film by Bruce Dern. The first draft was 130 pages, had two protagonists, and took place over a three-year period. The God's truth version of the Madison story would have made a terrific documentary or a compelling magazine article. As a theatrical narrative, however, it was a difficult story to tell. (I still have a copy of the original draft in a box somewhere in the bowels of my house. I also have all of those taped interviews.)

As we proceeded on further drafts, we ended up doing a lot of compressing and combining. We shortened the period of time in which the story takes place from three years to one summer, and we combined our two protagonists (the team manager and the driver) into one lead character—the driver of the boat.

This was our only choice, as he was the guy who put his life on the line every time he climbed into the cockpit. The real team manager, Tony Steinhardt, was incredibly understanding given the fact that we took many of the conflicts and drama that he lived in the story and gave them to the character of our driver. Tony acted as the film's technical adviser, and went above and beyond the call of duty while we were shooting the film. I think he realized how difficult it was for us to get the project going, and simply swallowed his ego in the interest of the movie. *Madison* is his story as much as anyone's, so he's a hell of a guy to be so cool about it. I know he cries every time he sees the film, and I think it is the spirit of the story that he is getting caught up in.

There were a couple of important events in the true story that had taken place during the seasons prior to when our film takes place—we simply moved them into the summer in which our narrative plays out. My favorite moment of the movie is during the ending credits where we see the actual *ABC Wide World of Sports* footage playing out on half the screen as the credits roll. I have felt very strongly about doing this from the beginning. I think seeing how similar the real color film looks to our recreation goes a long way in eliminating the "cheese/cliché" factor that these underdog sports stories sometimes fall victim to. It seems that audiences are responding the same way to this footage—yes, David does beat Goliath, and yes, we have all seen this dozens of times before, but dagblamit, this really happened—stick around and take a look for yourself.

Q: *How do the people in this movie feel the adaptation works?*

A: I think what we were shooting for from the beginning was to capture the spirit of the *Madison* story. From the reactions of those involved in the real story, I believe we pulled it off. I think they know that this film could be great for the town, which does rely on tourism, and also be a boon to the relatively unknown sport of unlimited hydroplane racing. We had several hundred citizens of Madison at an advance screening, and their reaction was fantastic—cheers and tears and a standing ovation. I'm not sure we could have gotten a better endorsement than that.

Q: *What advice would you have for any writers doing adaptations?*

A: I think the first thing is to research the subject thoroughly, and then research it some more. Although we made some changes and fictionalized some things, many of our tweaks came from real stories (whether they happened to other characters in our sport, or outside of our time line, we found ways to incorporate them). The tragic death of our protagonist's close friend happened outside of our film's time frame, but was an important part of his life, so we moved it into our story. When the real characters watch our film, I truly believe the emotions we portray onscreen take them right back to the emotions they felt during their lives, regardless that we changed the years and the names.

I guess the other piece of advice would be not to give up if you feel passionate about your story. We met roadblocks at every step of the process from script to screen.

The Powers That Be told us, "Nice little script, but no one will make it."

Yet, we found someone to make it.

They told us, "You'll never be able to cast it. The story is too small."

Yet, Jim Caviezel chose it over many high-profile studio projects his agents were begging him to do. Bruce Dern liked the script so much that he postponed a planned hiatus to do it. And Jake Lloyd chose it as his follow-up to *Star Wars*, because he and his parents liked the character and the story.

And they told us, "It's a nightmare shooting combination— high-budget action, on water, with low-budget funding."

They were right, but we pulled it off.

Q: *In the end, what are the advantages and pitfalls involved in adapting a true-life story?*

A: Starting out, I think it would seem easier to do an adaptation, since the story has already happened. But I think it is more difficult than writing an original fiction story. Also, a lot depends on how long ago the story took place. In our case, most of the characters were still around, so we were putting words into existing people's mouths.

As a writer, these people are always standing over your shoulder reading as you type, and that is pretty daunting. One advantage is that the research is fun, particularly if you like the people you are working with and their story is inspiring (as was the case with *Madison*). Asking questions, running a tape recorder, and jotting notes is easy. Unfortunately, working all of that info into a compelling narrative that plays out in ninety-five minutes is not quite as fun. So many things that seem perfect during research are difficult to incorporate when it comes down to the screenplay. I guess in the end, the old saying is true: the only real writing is rewriting. I'm glad that *Madison* took so many years to find its way to the screen, because the script was simply not strong enough until the end of the process, after more than a decade of writing, encompassing dozens of drafts and thousands of pages.

• • •

Okay, now you have read Fred Farley's article about the Gold Cup and *Miss Madison*, as well as the interview of screenwriter Scott Bindley. What can be learned from looking at both? Let us start at the beginning.

The first significant step in adapting a story like this is finding the screen story inside the real story. In his article "*Miss Madison*, the Gold Cup Champion," Fred Farley says, "Miss Madison was not the thousand-to-one longshot of popular legend. On the contrary, she was a bona-fide contender."

Sure, there's still a story there, but clearly not as good a story, as emotionally involving a story as something like *Rocky*. We love to root for the underdog. What's more, the greater the obstacles our characters have to overcome, the greater their victory. The other factor in this equation is risk. The more the character risks, the more satisfying his triumph will be when those risks pay off. So the reality is that the screenwriter must crank up the story in the adaptation, inject it with nitrous oxide, and make it faster, funnier, and riskier. What really happened is important, but you must push it further if you want it to sing on the big screen.

Let's look at the main character's journey now. In real life, Jim McCormick had a lot at stake when he got into the *Miss Madison*. It was a risky sport, and the eyes of the world were focused upon him since this event was being covered by ABC's *Wide World of Sports*. Yet in the film there is so much more at risk. It is clearly put forward in the movie that Jim is risking the finances of the town, his marriage, his safety, his friendships, and a relationship with his son to drive the *Miss Madison*. He doesn't want to drive (a reluctant hero is always good), but he feels a duty to the town and a chance for his own redemption. If there's not a good turnout for the race, the town will go bankrupt. If he loses the race or, worse, doesn't even finish it, he proves all the naysayers and corporate teams right. The screenwriters do their damnedest to make sure we, the audience, know there's a lot riding on this guy.

In reality, Jim McCormick drove the *Miss Madison* for the entire year of 1971. This truth wouldn't make for a thrilling story. It's a better story to have Skip quit, have the new driver (Buddy) injured in another race, and have Jim, who hasn't driven in years, forced to come out of retirement to drive in the big race.

Let's look at another major story point that differs slightly in terms of what really happened versus how it was portrayed in the screenplay. The Gold Cup was held in Madison due to a misunderstanding and the fact that Madison's bid was the only one submitted on time. Once again, this is not bad. But why leave things to chance when you, as the author, have complete control over the story? In the film, Jim puts himself and the town on the spot by writing a bad $50,000 check to the APBA. He does it out of pride, and this act is a great way of showing that pride is one of his major traits. Jim knows there isn't enough money to cover the check, but his reputation and the reputation of his town are at stake, so he does it anyway and it's a great filmic moment.

Unlike novels and other adaptive catalysts, articles don't have an entire story. They've got the short version. That means you'll have to expand, and there's only one way to do it: research. While a lot can be gleaned from articles like Fred Farley's, there's no substitute for good ol'-fashioned legwork. Yes, you'll find that more often than not, folks are more than happy to talk to you about the event(s) you're researching. You can interview by phone, work back and forth over e-mail, or go visit the person. While the latter is the most expensive, it's generally the most rewarding. Sure, you can learn a lot over the phone, but there's a different connection when you're face to face. It really brings the story to life when you can see emotions in person. It's the difference between reading a screenplay and watching a movie. Talk to as many people as you can, get as many different points of view as possible. The more stories you have, the more material you have to work with.

The brothers Bindley both made several trips to Madison to interview the people who participated in the event. They talked to the key players and people who were around when the events took place. Of course, be aware that every person you talk to is going to recount the tale a bit differently. So whose story do you use? Who do you believe?

You take them all; you believe them all. Then you pick bits and pieces from all those tales and put them together. This is the best part of adaptation, of writing in general. No other part of the writing process is more exciting than conceiving the story, taking ideas from your research and your imagination, and molding them into something coherent, tangible.

Madison isn't a fact-for-fact account of the actual events. It's close, to be sure, but the art of adaptation is not a simple recounting of history. Details and facts are important, but they can be manipulated. You're writing a movie, not a magazine article. The adaptor's skill is measured by his ability to take the facts and shape them into a screenworthy tale. Don't be bound by the truth, but don't ignore it, either.

The fact is, truth in reality and truth in film are two different things. What we're trying to achieve is verisimilitude, the appearance of truth, which is to say that the situations, characters, and emotions of your story are true inside the world you create. When your story rings true to the ear and appears true to the audience you are writing for, you'll know you've succeeded.

Actually sitting down to interview someone should be one of the last steps of your research process. The more information you have before you go to the person(s), the more you can get from them. Find old newspaper articles, magazines, video footage, newscasts, anything that can give you information on your subject. Once you've amassed all the information you can, lay it all out.

Some folks use note cards, some plot all the information on huge sheets of butcher paper, some jot it down in a notebook, others use computer programs to organize their information. Whatever works best for you, the important thing is to have a system that allows you to see and sort through all of the data, facts, and stories you've compiled. Now you can start to shape your story.

Find the one word that encapsulates it: love, honor, pride, revenge, loss, and so on. Start forming your idea with that. Eliminate the events that don't support your idea. Now define your story in a sentence. Tell yourself what your story is. It doesn't have to be precise, just the basic idea. For *Madison* you could say, "An underdog hydroplane racing team beats all the odds and wins the big race." That's what the story's about.

The next step is to find a sentence that describes the story in terms of other films. This is as helpful to the writer as it is to the agent reading your synopsis. Its importance to you, the author, is that it gives you a source of comparison and reference. If you said that *Madison* was *Rocky* meets *Days of Thunder* on the hydroplane unlimited circuit, you're not just describing it to others, you're describing it to yourself. You can see what went wrong and what went right in the other films. It forces you to find ways to be different. Not different for the sake of being different, but different to avoid duplicating other films while still maintaining a thematic similarity and emotional sincerity that worked in preexisting movies.

Okay, now you're ready to move on to Professor K.'s Big Seven for *Madison*.

The Big Seven: *Madison*

1. *Who is the main character?*

   Jim McCormick.

2. *What does Jim want/need/desire?*

   He wants to save the town, save his family and marriage, win the big race, and most importantly, have the love of his son. In more specific terms, he wants to win the APBA Gold Cup to prove to the world, himself, and his son that he's not a loser, and neither is his town or the people who live in it.

3. *Who/what keeps him from achieving what he wants?*

   Miss Madison, the town's racing boat, is always breaking down. The town doesn't have the money to sponsor the contest or fix the boat. His obsession with the Miss Madison is alienating him from his family. He's not the driver he once was.

4. *How in the end does Jim achieve what he wants in an unexpected, interesting, and unusual way?*

The town rallies behind him. The pit crew steals parts from an old airplane in front of another town's city hall. The old crew chief helps them get the nitrous oxide kit on the boat to work. He places a lucky third in the second heat without taxing the motor. In the final lap, he uses the nitro and flies past the *Miss Budweiser*.

5. *What are you trying to say by ending the story this way?*

   With hard work, perseverance, and an indomitable spirit, you can overcome anything.

6. *How is the story told?*

   The story is told chronologically with flashbacks.

7. *How do your main character and any supporting characters change over the course of the story?*

   Jim gets his confidence and self-respect back by fulfilling his dream and overcoming his fear of driving. Mike learns to be proud of his father and his town. Bonnie finds the love and faith in her husband that she had when they were first married. The town has a renewed sense of accomplishment and pride.

   The next step is the following scene-o-gram.

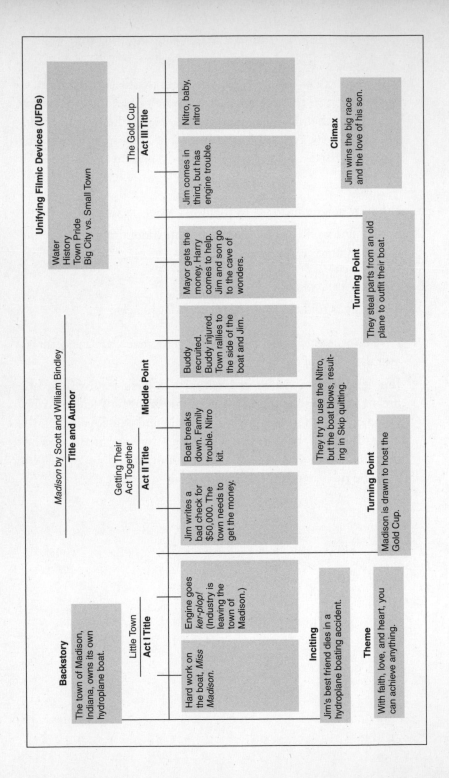

Backstory

The town of Madison, Indiana, owns its own hydroplane boat.

Madison by Scott and William Bindley

Title and Author

Unifying Filmic Devices (UFDs)

Water
History
Town Pride
Big City vs. Small Town

Little Town
Act I Title

Getting Their Act Together
Act II Title

The Gold Cup
Act III Title

Hard work on the boat, *Miss Madison.*

Engine goes *ker-plop!* (Industry is leaving the town of Madison.)

Jim writes a bad check for $50,000. The town needs to get the money.

Boat breaks down. Family trouble. Nitro kit.

Middle Point

Buddy recruited. Buddy injured. Town rallies to the side of the boat and Jim.

Mayor gets the money. Harry comes to help. Jim and son go to the cave of wonders.

Jim comes in third, but has engine trouble.

Nitro, baby, nitro!

Climax

Jim wins the big race and the love of his son.

Inciting

Jim's best friend dies in a hydroplane boating accident.

Theme

With faith, love, and heart, you can achieve anything.

Turning Point

Madison is drawn to host the Gold Cup.

They try to use the Nitro, but the boat blows, resulting in Skip quitting.

Turning Point

They steal parts from an old plane to outfit their boat.

10

Learning by Writing Across the Genres

Case Study: *Glengarry Glen Ross*

This is mainly a screenwriting book, but one thing I hope it conveys is how a screenwriter must think of herself as not just a screenwriter, but also a playwright, poet, or novelist. In other words, if you are a writer whose medium of choice is screenwriting, the other genres are options that you should consider, especially for certain stories that might in fact be better off told in those mediums.

I've had the opportunity to help a lot of people with their writing across a variety of genres (screenplays, short stories, novels, plays, articles) over the years. Occasionally, I'll read someone's work and find that he is really writing something completely different from what he intends. I'll read someone's short story and think, "That's not a short story, that's a play." It happens more often than you might think. Novels that should be short stories, screenplays that should be novels, short stories that should be plays. No one ever really wants to hear that what he's written would be better suited to a different form. But it's not all bad. In fact, it might turn out to be a blessing. Believe it or not, it's easier to get a play performed or a novel published than it is to sell a screenplay. Heck, all you need to put on your play are actors and a place for them to act. You might not make any money, but you get to taste the fruits of your labor, which can be as sweet and juicy as you've imagined.

So if you are told that you need to try retelling your tale in a new medium, embrace that opportunity. Trust me, it's better to have a stage play or novel that you can sell than to have tried to force the story into screenplay form only to be told over and over again,

"Sorry, but this feels too small and not visual enough for a film—WE PASS!"

In general, smaller, character-driven stories are often quite hard to sell in Hollywood. However, smaller novels and stage plays often succeed in those genres. And if your novel is published or your play is produced, all of a sudden you have a work that has been validated in another medium and thus represents a safer choice for the Hollywood buyers, who are always trying to better their odds for success. You might even have a script already written based upon the story of the novel you just got published, and when Hollywood comes a-knocking on your door for the film rights, you can get paid to write the script (which means you can take a three-month paid vacation in France and upon your return submit your screenplay, which was written years earlier, but everything in Hollywood thinks you struggled with it for months).

This then leads me to a discussion of a successful Off-Broadway play of mine, *Boychik*, which I transformed into a screenplay entitled *Lawrence of Suburbia*. The history of *Lawrence of Suburbia* is a wonderful example of how being open to adaptations can lead to wonderful and unexpected things for any writer. Let me start at the beginning and lead you on a journey across many years, many drafts, and many genres, illuminating my path through the world of adaptations and the many lessons I've learned along the way.

Years ago I taught a course at USC entitled "Writing Across the Genres." In this course, all the students were required to start by writing a poem. Then they were asked to take this poem and its central images and themes and transpose them into a short story. Next they were asked to take some of the dialogue, language, metaphors, and themes from this short story and use them as a basis for a one-act play. In the last few weeks of class, for their final exam, they adapted the play into a short film script, still incorporating the central themes, images, metaphors, and symbols accumulated in the writing of the original poem, short story, and play. The students seemed to really take to this course. In addition, it has played a central role in my artistic life as well, in that I have used it as a model for developing much of my work since then.

In fact, my film screenplay *Lawrence of Suburbia* is a real-life example of this adaptation process in action. *Lawrence of Suburbia* was at first inspired by a long poem I wrote called *Living Inside a Safety Deposit Box in the Back of the Bank of America*. This poem dealt with my fears of death and loss. It featured a central image of its protagonist opening up his father's safety deposit box and crawling inside to ensure that he will never have to deal with death and always remain safe. It also featured a powerful segment based upon an early-morning ride in the Connecticut countryside in which the foggy road was littered with the dead bodies of several possums. The sight of all these dead possums on the road was a powerful image that I knew was destined to find its way into my work. I juxtaposed the safety deposit box metaphor with the possum metaphor, and out came a poem.

This poem turned out to be one of my favorites, and I knew there was more gold in "them thar hills" that had yet to be mined. So I moved forward, turning the poem into a short story. I had problems with this adaptation, since this poem, as most poems are, was rather ethereal and nonnarrative. There were powerful images and metaphors, but there was no story, no plot, no clear throughline on which to hang the story. But I plugged away at it anyway.

The very act of pushing this poem into a story was highly illuminating. I was finally seeing, really seeing, what distinguished one genre from another. What worked, what was in fact expected in a poem, was also, by its very nature, not conducive to a short story. I could transfer an idea or an image easily, but a short story by its very definition requires more than just a few neat turns of phrase and cool descriptions. I had to find my story and nail it before I could go any further. So I began to invent and play. I wasn't threatened by the act of creation. I embraced it and learned to see what my unconscious would do with what had started as a little poem about my fears of death and dead possums.

To be honest, the short story never seemed to work. I was still too close to the poem and really never achieved clarity as to what my story really was about. But I had discovered my sensitive and likable protagonist, Lawrence, who was on a spiritual journey, and I also began to flesh out where the story needed to go if it was ever to have any legs.

The best thing that came from writing the short story was the introduction of a long childhood scene that beautifully encapsulated the father-and-son motif that seemed to dominate this piece. The heart of this scene was a moving story about Lawrence and his father playing Ping-Pong that was inspired by a friend who told me that the saddest moment of his life was the day he beat his father at Ping-Pong. Not the day he lost, for his father was a very strong player and he was used to losing to him, but the day he finally got good enough to beat his own father. This also proved to be the day he realized his father was human, and therefore mortal.

In a true, poignant addendum to this story, my friend's father really did die at a young age, only a few years after that fateful Ping-Pong match and the inception of my story. In retrospect, what strikes me most about the series of events that occurred as I created Lawrence was the synchronicity of the emergence of thematically linked stories that all seemed to appear in my life as I most needed them.

I'm not trying to get weird or metaphysical here. It just seems to me that if you as a writer are open to the stories, images, and symbols that are already in existence in the world around you, you will see them and then can incorporate them into your work, weaving a seemingly incoherent tapestry into a coherent whole.

Without getting too New-Agey mystical, talk to writers and a majority will agree that sure, writer's block exists, but there's also a counterforce, a magical energy at work in the universe that seems to send you the stories you need when you are ready to receive them. You just have to be open to them. And many times, the best way to open your windows and to experience the thrill of the new is to do an adaptation in a new medium.

Now, let's get back to *Lawrence*. The short story was interesting to me, but didn't really seem to be of interest to anyone else. However, I had just recently finished writing a big-budget play that everyone seemed to love, but that everyone also claimed was just too darned expensive to mount. For my next play, I vowed to create a piece that was pure theater of the imagination, a simple-to-mount, single-actor project that no one could say was too expensive. One that didn't revolve around costumes, sets, actors, or props. One that was basically a performer and his story. And that was when my safety deposit box story leaped back to mind.

I could rewrite this story as a monodrama in which a single actor pulled several props out of his father's safety deposit box and in doing so use each prop as a vehicle to stimulate specific stories of his life with his father. With the flick of his wrist, the actor could whip out a Ping-Pong paddle and the audience could be thrown back twenty years into the world of father-son Ping-Pong matches. This is the magic of theater. No costume changes, no big set changes, just a flick of a light and the actor is now a boy poised to return his father's Ping-Pong serve.

So the core story of *Lawrence* flew back into my life in the form of a one-man show. As I started writing the play, I knew I was on to something that was highly workable. The short story provided a great seed for several scenes, but alas, I needed more. I delved into my past, and new scenes for the play seemed to materialize simply and quickly. The director pushed me harder and harder to dredge up real stories from my past. I wrote a whole series of tales that directly stemmed from childhood memories I hadn't thought of in years, and proved to be perfect additions.

One traumatic experience in my teenage years of attempting to write a college essay became a major moment in the play, embodied by a simple silver Cross ballpoint pen. A moment of stress during a Little League ball game became the centerpiece for a long baseball sequence that tied in nicely with the already preexisting Ping-Pong drama. Yes, the play was really coming together nicely. We mounted it in a series of staged readings and were getting tremendous responses from audiences.

It was my life, but it wasn't. It was the life of a character torn from my life, but distinctly different from me. It was the life of Lawrence Levin, a suburban man-child searching for truth, the love of his father, and religious redemption. The play, which was initially called *Yahrzeit*, was produced in Los Angeles and ran for six sold-out months. It was doing so well, there was interest in doing an Off-Broadway run, where it was renamed *Boychik*. After that, the play was produced occasionally around the country, but now it is essentially finished and stuck on my shelf.

For years I considered adapting it into a screenplay, but every time I tried, it seemed to defy adaptation. I had spent over seven years taking it from poem to story to play script, and I was too close to it to do the adaptation. Every word seemed sacred and I was just not ready to fool with it. So I put it away, convinced it had run its course and lived a good, long life . . .

That is, until my new manager urged me to write a screenplay based on the *Boychik* play script. She had read most of my work and was certain that this piece was the one thing I had written that was truly closest to my heart. So I agreed to engage in the process of adaptation once again and give it a shot. It would be easy, right? I knew the story better than anybody, and all I had to do was plug it into screenplay format, spruce it up a bit, and I'd be done. One easy little job and I'd have myself a film script.

I wrote the script in a month and handed it to my manager only to be told, "Sorry, but it's just not there yet. It's still too small, too talky, too much like a play. Open it up. Raise the stakes. Make it more visual. MAKE IT INTO A MOVIE."

She was right, of course. So I did another rewrite, only to be greeted with the same response. This went on for over a year. Then, another. Little did I know when I first started that I would be spending the next two years of my life doing this final little, easy adaptation.

By the eighth draft and the end of the second year, I was ready to quit, and I was convinced my manager was sick of me and this script. When she called me into her office, I was sure she was ready to let me go as a client. I felt like an inept loser who couldn't write. But when I arrived at her office, she greeted me with a big smile and congratulated me, saying, "Awesome. You finally nailed it."

The script was not a play any longer, it was really a movie with a life of its own. The characters had shed their theatrical skins and moved into a more visual world. The characters who were merely mentioned in passing in the play had lives of their own. They had quirks and passions. They breathed and farted and swore. The main character's dramatic problem in the play was merely a religious dilemma hinged upon his relationship with his father, but now in the script, it became much more complex.

In the final screenplay, in the first act Lawrence's marriage was put into jeopardy, as was his job. His relationships were deepened and new characters were added. Scenes that were merely mentioned or alluded to were now fully played out, and of course new scenes were invented to fill in the holes that now existed. It took me eight drafts because I needed that many to fully let go of the theatrical elements and embrace the new filmic elements. Even some of my favorite moments from the play, including the possum death scene that had survived from the original poem written years earlier, had to be lost due to the constraints of the new story that had emerged in the screenplay.

I knew the story better than anyone else, but still, I had to let go of it and see it anew as a screenplay. I had to ask myself, how will I structure this so it works for a filmgoing audience? Flashbacks that are smooth and effortless onstage can be fatal to a screenplay. The play itself lasted 75 minutes onstage, but the movie had to be 105 minutes long. I had to get the story going faster in the script and lose all elements that weren't essential to pushing that story forward.

And so I did. Not at first, but in pieces over the course of eight drafts. And I believe that as a result of developing this story in and through several mediums, I learned more and more about what I was really trying to say. Now the 105-page screenplay that is finally finished represents a very strong and beautiful, fully realized dramatization of a little two-page poem I wrote about a kid hiding in his father's safety deposit box.

I hope my diatribe about my personal experiences with adaptations has shed some light on the major issues I'm trying to deal with in this text. Clearly, the act of adaptation entails differences based upon the medium that is being adapted. For example, adapting novels is generally a matter of compressing and cutting material to fit the original story into a screenplay. Short story adaptations involve expansion and scene addition to make the tale big enough and long enough for the screen. Play adaptations are similar to short stories in terms of expansion, but there's a major difference: plays are dialogue-heavy.

In other words, plays live or die by the quality of their dialogue. The locations in which the scenes take place are limited by necessity. You can't jump from place to place on the stage as you can in a screenplay. There just isn't the time or room for that many sets. Yes, you can move from place to place via props and dialogue, you can describe where you are, but you can't actually go or be there. In fact, sometimes, you can even break the cardinal rule of storytelling in playwriting. You can, owing to the constraints of the stage, sometimes TELL INSTEAD OF SHOW! But you can never do this in screenwriting. As a filmic writer, you must always expand the story, always make it big enough to fill the screen.

Depending on how long the play you're working with is, you've got anywhere from a half-hour to two hours of the spoken word. The good news is that you've got lots of great dialogue to pick from. The bad news is that your dialogue usually takes place in a very limited amount of different locations. Watch the first thirty minutes of any movie. You might have twenty different locations. That's the dilemma.

And let's be honest here, there are some plays that have an inherent inclination toward the screen. This, then, brings us to exploring a major Pulitzer Prize–winning play, David Mamet's *Glengarry Glenn Ross*, which featured dialogue, scenes, and characters ripe for a filmic adaptation. If you have not seen *Glengarry Glen Ross*, put this book down. I command you, go to your local video rental store. Rent it, watch it . . . I'll wait here.

If you're reading this, you've now seen David Mamet's *Glengarry Glen Ross*. What was your favorite scene? I don't have any oracular powers, but 9.9 times out of 10, Alec Baldwin's sales speech is the favorite. No wonder: It's a brilliant piece of writing. The most frequently quoted lines of the film come from that speech. You can imagine how concerned Mamet must have been when he was adapting his play to the screen. A writer certainly doesn't want to cut a speech of that caliber.

SURPRISE! That scene's not in the original play at all. Why was it added? Forget about the fact that the play just wasn't quite long enough. Of course it tacked on some much-needed minutes to the film. The answer to the question lies in the nature of stories for the stage and stories for the screen. Plays are about speech, the rhythm of it, the pace, verbiage, patterns, and repetitions of it. Scenes, plot, and structure are secondary.

Screenwriting is about story, plot, structure, character, and then dialogue. Dialogue can make or break a film as well, but not in the same way that it affects the stage. The story is what brings people to the cineplex. If the dialogue isn't that great but the story is interesting and original, the film will still probably make money. The dialogue in *The Matrix* was a tragedy, but it was a hell of an interesting concept and it made a ton of money. Mamet himself once said, "The imperative of structure and story was driven home to me when I began to write for the movies."

That's why the sales conference scene was added to the film. Without it there is no catalyst, no real motivation (aside from frustration) for the characters' actions. The sales contest is in the play, but it's just there. It's not the insult to the men that it is in the film. The men are upset about it, but Mitch and Murray don't send down the hard-nosed Alec Baldwin character to push the point home in the play. Baldwin's character's treatment of the sales force would insult any working man. It would be the straw that broke the back of the man carrying the camel. We as the audience identify with that. The story for the screen needed that turn, that catalyst, to set the actions of the characters in motion.

Blake, Baldwin's character, really gets Moss (Ed Harris) riled up and seems to target him in particular, probably because Moss won't shut his yap. Aaranow (Alan Arkin) is insulted, but lacks the moxie to really say or do anything. His weakness is magnified by Blake's speech, and that opens him up to Moss's machinations. Levene (Jack Lemmon) is more devastated than insulted. He's got a daughter in the hospital and bills mounting. This man has to sell, period. He's desperate. Ricky Roma (Al Pacino) isn't at the sales conference because he's busy selling in the bar. He's on the top of the board anyway, and as we find out, he's already got the premium leads because he's selling Glengarry real estate.

The addition of Blake and his speech sets the story rolling. The speech affects Shelly Levene more than it affects anyone else. If this story has a main character, it's Levene, but we'll come back to that. I've said that expansion is the name of the game in the play-to-screenplay adaptation. That means a lot when we talk in terms of location. The play has two locations: Act One is in a Chinese restaurant, Act Two is in the office. Needless to say, two locations don't exactly cut it for a feature film. *Glengarry* the screenplay doesn't really have all that many locations in the film, either, but it definitely has more than the play. It has scenes in the Chinese restaurant, the office, the alley, the phone booth, Moss's car, another bar, the exterior of the office, and the client's house (the one Levene gets booted out of).

That's certainly not a lot of locations, but it is more than the play has, and the change of locations gives the story a more cinematic feel. Mamet found a way to broaden the story with new locations and a few new scenes, yet managed to keep almost all of his dialogue from the play. As I've said before, this kind of adaptation doesn't involve as much cutting as a novel would. The trick is to figure out how to keep, or rather how to use, the strong play dialogue in the screenplay.

When I was adapting *Boychik* into the screenplay *Lawrence of Suburbia*, I found that I could convert a lot of the main character's (Lawrence) dialogue into the description. Granted, no one (except those reading the script) will see those lines of dialogue I've converted to description when it's on the screen. But it was a way to keep some of the work I'd done and at the same time let go of the dialogue.

Mamet worked the dialogue he had in the two play locations into several other locations. He added some dialogue for length and for story. But the most important thing here is that he kept the essence of the play intact. The heart of the screenplay pumped the same blood as the play, the body just had to be worked out and buffed up. Never forget that what made the play successful was the dialogue. Do not abandon it. Instead, do what you can to help the screenplay embrace it.

The core of this story is the transformation of Shelly Levene. You might say it's the resurrection and reburial of Shelly Levene. He's a salesman who's been in the business for a long time and has lost his edge. He's the only one without a single sale on the board. His daughter's very sick, and he needs the money to pay for her hospital stay. Not only that, but he desperately wants to reclaim his past glory.

Levene tries his damnedest to squeeze some of the new Glengarry leads out of Williamson (Kevin Spacey), but it's a no-go. He hits the leads he has and miracle of all miracles, he makes a huge sale to Bruce and Harriet Nyborg. It's a bona fide miracle. Now he's got the chance to tell Williamson off, and he does. Williamson deserves an arse-chewing, but it leads to Levene's undoing. Levene's on top of the world one minute, back on track using the old ways, but things quickly fall apart on him. Williamson latches on to something Levene says and gets him to confess that he ripped off the place.

As if that isn't bad enough, he finds out that the huge sale he had wouldn't have amounted to diddley-squat. The Nyborgs don't have any money; they're known deadbeats, and the check isn't going to be any good. Williamson knew it and he gave Shelly the lead anyway. It's lose-lose all around. If he hadn't robbed the office, he'd be no better off than he was the day before. The Nyborgs' check would have bounced, and he'd still be broke, disheartened, and at the bottom of the board. And just when there was a sparkle of hope for Shelly.

Ouch! That David Mamet tells some dark, tragic tales. There's a lot of ambiguity in this story, a lot of information that's kept from us. This isn't generally what we see in film. Sure, some things are left to the audience, but for the most part we know what the score is. That's a rule of thumb that has to bend a little when you're adapting a Pulitzer Prize–winning play like *Glengarry Glen Ross*. Every play is different, and the adaptation of this one is an interesting model. Study it, learn from it.

If you're adapting one of your own plays or someone else's, always remember that the key is expansion. Make your characters big enough to fill the screen and make your story big enough to fill the seats. Now let's see how the film *Glengarry Glen Ross* breaks down.

The Big Seven: *Glengarry Glen Ross*

1. *Who is the main character?*
   Shelly Levene.

2. *What does Shelly want/need/desire?*
   He wants to help his daughter, he wants to get the good leads, but more than anything, he wants to be the man he once was, a leading salesman.

3. *Who/what keeps Shelly from getting what he wants?*
   Williamson has the leads and he's not giving Shelly anything to work with. Blake questions his manhood in the sales meeting. He doesn't have money to buy any leads from Williamson. He's lost his confidence as a salesman.

4. *How does he get what he wants in an unexpected/interesting/ unusual way?*
   He robs the office and sells the leads to Jerry Graff with Moss. He makes an unbelievable sale to the Nyborgs that gives him his confidence back. It is, however, all for naught. Williamson figures out he robbed the place, and even if he hadn't, the Nyborgs' check would have bounced.

5. *What is Mamet trying to say by ending the story this way?*
   However sorry we might feel for Levene, we need to remember that he has been in this racket for God knows how many years. Imagine how many lives he has destroyed with his lies. Sooner or later, what goes around comes around. There's also something to be said for the desperation of someone in a dead-end job with a

boss who hates him and a profession that eventually leads to moral bankruptcy. In his purest form, Levene is just a guy trying to make ends meet the best way he knows how. Can we really fault him for what he does? Mamet said that his objective with this play was to "create a closed moral universe and to leave the evaluation to the audience."

6. *How is the story told?*

Chronologically, no voice-over, no flashback.

7. *How do the main character and any other characters change over the course of the story?*

Levene regains his confidence and gets some cash by selling the leads, but everything he's gained is taken away when Williamson figures him out. He's back to square one.

Moss is the same old conniving, self-involved jackass he's always been. Only now he's going to be a conniving, self-involved jackass in jail.

Aaronow is the same stammering shell of a man he always was, but it's been proven that perhaps his will is stronger than we thought. After all, he didn't go in on Moss's little scheme.

Roma is right where he was, with the exception of the fact that he's not $6,000 richer as a result of Williamson's blowing his deal.

Williamson sure hasn't changed, but he did prove (not only to himself, but to Shelly) that he knows a thing or two about the fine art of negotiation.

Not many of the characters have much of an arc. The character who comes the closest to the kind of arc we generally see in a screenplay is Levene. But Mamet remained true to the essence of the original play. It wasn't about change, or even a need for change. It was more or less, *Hey, this is how things are for these guys. What do you think?*

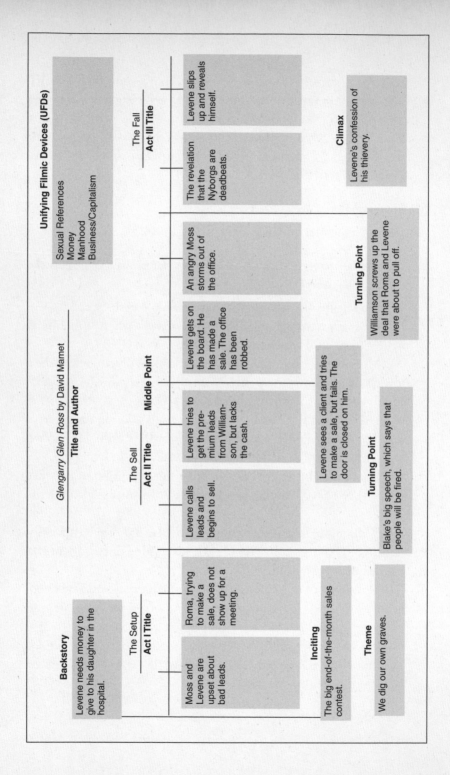

Unifying Filmic Devices (UFDs)
Sexual References
Money
Manhood
Business/Capitalism

Glengarry Glen Ross by David Mamet
Title and Author

Backstory
Levene needs money to give to his daughter in the hospital.

The Setup
Act I Title

The Sell
Act II Title

The Fall
Act III Title

Middle Point

Moss and Levene are upset about bad leads.

Roma, trying to make a sale, does not show up for a meeting.

Levene calls leads and begins to sell.

Levene tries to get the premium leads from Williamson, but lacks the cash.

Levene gets on the board. He has made a sale. The office has been robbed.

An angry Moss storms out of the office.

The revelation that the Nyborgs are deadbeats.

Levene slips up and reveals himself.

Inciting
The big end-of-the-month sales contest.

Theme
We dig our own graves.

Turning Point
Blake's big speech, which says that people will be fired.

Levene sees a client and tries to make a sale, but fails. The door is closed on him.

Turning Point
Williamson screws up the deal that Roma and Levene were about to pull off.

Climax
Levene's confession of his thievery.

154

11

Good, Evil, and the Eternal Combat Over Adaptations

Case Study: *X-Men*

Enter a world where the impossible is commonplace, where eyes fire lasers and see through clothes—er, walls. Here, steel-tendoned arms level buildings and lob cars like Ping-Pong balls. Onomatopoeias—*KATHOOM*—explode off the page and—*SWACK*—slap you in the face. Good and evil are locked in eternal combat, and the fate of the world eternally hangs in the balance. Yes, the comic universe is a treacherous and wondrous place.

This genre may be one of the most difficult to adapt. There may be hundreds of issues of the same title and a multitude of spinoffs, dozens of characters, and countless story lines to take into consideration. The conventions of each world are thoroughly established, and thus your missteps will stick out like sore thumbs in a room full of hand amputees. But there is hope in this bold undertaking, true believers: Professor K. and the Big Seven are here to save the day.

Before we charge headlong into this business of comic book adaptation, let's chat about the legal issues regarding this particular genre. Odds are that Marvel will not give you the rights to make a Silver Surfer movie. Sure, they'd sell them to you, but you can't afford them (if you can, please write the check out to me and I'll be sure it gets to the right people . . .). But you don't need the rights just to write a screenplay. You will need the permission of the material's owner if you want to make any money selling it, however. Although it can be a wonderful exercise to try and pull this off. And then, hey, let's say you write an unbelievable Incredible Hulk script and send it to Marvel. Maybe they love it and decide to buy it from you. It has happened. Or they could also throw it in the garbage and you might never hear from them again. That's the risk you take when you develop material based upon characters that are not public domain and not owned by you.

All right, all right, I can hear you clamoring, "What's the point of doing a comic book adaptation if I can't even send it out when I'm done? Am I just supposed to write for fun?" God bless you if you are. But there's a more practical solution to this problem. Go to the smaller, independent comic book authors and publishers. There's an untapped well of adaptation oil waiting for you there. There are literally hundreds of titles to choose from. Better yet, these are stories and characters that the moviegoing public hasn't seen yet. The big Hollywood hit *The Mask* was based on a little miniseries of comics published by the independent comic publisher Dark Horse.

Now, here's the best part: Many of these independents are more than willing to let you write about their characters. Refer to chapter 3 and use the boilerplate forms that I gave you to pursue some free options on material that you are excited about. Another thing you may wish to consider (if you only want to play with the big boys like Marvel and DC) is focusing on lesser-known characters, or at least less popular characters. *Blade* never generated huge sales as a comic character and probably still doesn't. But it made for a pretty damn entertaining two hours onscreen. Just fair warning, folks. If you want to harvest the fruits of your labors, pick your seeds carefully.

Compared to other genres, comics may be the most similar to screenplays, the difference being that the action is presented in stills, instead of just descriptive language. Regardless of the similarities, there are many questions to be answered. Is the comic you want to adapt team-based (*X-Men*, *The Fantastic Four*), or does it revolve around a single hero (*Superman*, *Blade*, *Batman*)? If it is team-based, who will the main character be (remember, there can only be one)?

Where will your story start? Will you start with the characters getting his superpowers (their origin), or will you start in the middle of the hero's career? Does your character even have superpowers, and if so, what are they and how can their strengths and weaknesses be used to maximum effect in the story? Who will the antagonist be? Are you using a story line from the comic, or creating your own? How faithful will you remain to the comic? Furthermore, what are the ramifications of changing the character or the conventions of his world? You owe nothing to the original material, but where should you take your liberties and where should you stick closely to the story?

Good questions all. Let's use X-Men (a film that was a critical and financial success) as an example. Our selection has now been made, and the comic we are adapting is team-based. So, how do we select our main character? Which character in this superhero squad is the most compelling and dynamic? Who, more than any other, do we want to see overcome tremendous obstacles to achieve a desirable goal? In our example, X-Men, Wolverine (Logan) was chosen. Why him?

1. He is the most popular of this particular superhero cadre, and as such the most commercially viable.
2. Much of his history, particularly his origins, is unknown. This gives a tremendous amount of latitude to the writer. No origin is known, so there is no inconsistency to worry about in that respect.
3. Taking into consideration the other characters who inhabit his world, Wolverine's powers are very limited. He has no eye lasers or superstrength. He's the most human and the easiest for a viewer to identify with.
4. He's a grumpy loner with a heart of gold, and man, do we love this type of guy. It's a proven formula. Look at any of the score of cop movies, martial arts flicks, and Die Hard knockoffs that we've gone to see over and over again.
5. Due to his personality traits (the most important being that he cares about virtually no one but himself), he has the potential for a more profound character arc than any of his compatriots.

And so, there we go. We now have a main character. Moreover, we have reasons to back up our choice, and we've answered the first question of the Big Seven. Obviously, with the lone hero story, the question of who the main character will be is a moot point. Now that we know who the story's about, we can move on to the question of where his story starts.

A man with no origin is a man of mystery. Logan is such a man. That gives us the freedom to start wherever we choose. Wolvie is introduced to us in a wire cage drinking, smoking, and fighting for money. Our boy's got nowhere to go but up. There's no better place to start. Was this just some arbitrary location the writer plucked out of the air while he was reading the trades and sitting on the toilet? No, this is where research comes in. Sure, you could just make something up, but taking this tidbit of Logan's known history and dropping it in early on lends an authenticity that fans of the comic will be looking for. Although I don't know that "looking for" is quite strong enough for what the fans will be doing. It's more like a seek-and-destroy mission to discredit the author of the screenplay and damn him for the debacle he's made of their beloved comic. As we discussed earlier in the *Harry Potter* chapter, one must tread very lightly when adapting the sacred work of an established pop culture phenom. So, then, the very thing that makes the material attractive to the movie business—the material's iconic status in the culture—will be the death of you as a screenwriter if you are not careful.

We do, however, see the origins of other characters, namely Magneto and Rogue. The origins of Cyclops and Storm were in the original draft of the screenplay as well, but they were cut, as they didn't necessarily add anything to the story. Plus, that leaves some extra candy for the sequel. Marvel recently published a series of comics detailing the origins of Wolverine, their thought being that if they didn't do it first, Twentieth Century Fox would.

It is important to note here that we do not need to open the screenplay with the main character. This applies not only to screenwriting, but to any story. Let's take a moment to talk about the opening scene of *X-Men*. I don't believe that any comic adaptation has ever opened with a scene this powerful and effective. The writing here is as intense as the visual it precedes. It's a confident prose, and we as readers have no doubt that this writer knows his business. These are the first few paragraphs of the opening scene.

Ext. Camp—Day

UP ON the door of a weathered cattle car as a German soldier steps into frame wearing that familiar gray of the all-too-familiar era.

He throws the door to reveal a mass of huddled and frightened people inside.

The words are not necessary. The language is not ours and the images say enough.

Men, women, and children are herded off the train like cattle toward a large open yard. There they huddle until the Germans begin to shout and shove through the mob.

The third paragraph is what really sets this apart: "The words are not necessary. The language is not ours and the images say enough." That's confidence in your prose and your story, and he's right. Now, consider what this scene does for the story.

It drops us headlong into the harshest of realities. This happened, the Holocaust is part of our history, and we are in the real world, not a stylized version of it (such as in *Batman*). The world is not a kind place, and as a young Magneto finds out, no one is coming to save him. Thus, after seeing the origin of Magneto, we understand the reasons why he is so driven not to allow a mutant holocaust. Perhaps the most important accomplishment of this scene is that it sets the tone with such authority. This is a serious place with serious consequences. It is not a completely dark tale, but it doesn't have onomatopoeic icons popping up, either.

We have our main character, we know where his story begins, now we need to know what he can do. Sure, you know what his powers are (you're writing it), the fans know what his powers are, but the reader may not. Every aspect needs to be introduced to the audience as though they know absolutely nothing. The comic book industry is one that relies on a clear and creative presentation of action, and it's through action that we give the reader what she needs to know. Show, don't tell, that is the law. So let it be written, so let it be done.

Film is a visual medium. The sooner we know what our hero can do, the better. *X-Men* establishes Wolverine's abilities in his first scenes, and it establishes them through action. He is up against a powerful opponent who seems twice the size of him, yet he knocks him unconscious in the ring with a minimum of effort. Woo-weee, our boy Wolvie can fight!

The real kicker comes when he pops his adamantium claws and cuts a shotgun in half. The writer has established his prowess in combat and his ability to heal, but he's also done something much more important. In this single action, he's made a very important statement about Logan's character. He will not back down; he will never surrender. But he's not a murderer. He could have just gutted the barkeep and the knife-wielding moron. It's imperative to establish who the characters are early on. It's the only way to know where they have to go and how they have to change by the end of our story. Now we know that Logan is a hard man; he's a fighter, but not a murderer. *Blade* and *Batman* establish their heroes' respective abilities in their first scenes as well.

So, let us look at the Big Seven.

1. *Who is the main character?*

Logan/Wolverine

2. *What does Logan/Wolverine want/need/desire?*

Let's start with the external. Logan wants to save Rogue and stop Magneto from turning the world's leaders into mutants (and thereby killing them). External goals are easy to spot, but they're always motivated by internal needs and desires.

At first Logan refuses to give Rogue a ride when he finds her in his trailer, but his compassion gets the better of him. As their relationship grows throughout the story, Logan sees the loner and outsider in himself also embodied in Rogue. He wants to keep her from becoming what he has become. She's just a child, and her "gift" has isolated her from humanity. Logan becomes a friend and father figure to Rogue, and when Magneto kidnaps her, we know there will be a reckoning. The important thing here, though, is that in helping and teaching Rogue, Logan starts to regain his own humanity and sense of compassion.

Here's where a real storyteller steps above the countless others who try, but inevitably fail. There's not just one thing that our main character wants or just one thing that he struggles with. When we give our characters issues and difficulties in every area of their lives, we create depth. Logan is also in love with Jean Grey, although he knows it can never work out between them. He knows nothing of his past except for the horrid bits and pieces that wrench him from sleep. He does not get along with the team leader (who's also Jean's boyfriend), Cyclops, and he really doesn't side with either Magneto or Charles Xavier. He exists in a lonely world somewhere between these two powerful leaders. His philosophy has been simple up until this point: cover your own ass. Last, but not least, he lives in a broken-down camper.

These are things we can all relate to: unrequited love, trying to find meaning in our lives, choosing sides, being forced to live a life we feel is beneath us. I know that in the 1970s, when I was stuck living out of my AMC Gremlin, following the Grateful Dead, and picking up cans for their deposit value, I believed that I really should be living in a Winnebago . . . sorry . . . more info than you need.

The point is, when we give our characters this kind of depth, we're one step closer to verisimilitude, the appearance of truth. Movies are not real. They are fabrications, fiction, fantasy. Even if it's an account of an actual event, it's merely a representation of the past reality. But if we as writers do it right, if we spin our tales with heart, clarity, and passion, if we fill our characters with the right amounts of love, lust, hate, humor, pride, greed, want, worry, and everything else that makes us human, if we push our stories to be real inside their worlds, then maybe, just maybe, our tales will have the appearance of truth, and for two hours an audience will pay good money to witness the tapestry we have woven. To them, it might really even seem real.

The character aspect of this concept is that the hopes, fears, and actions of our players need to make sense in the reality of their world. How well you craft your characters will determine how well you represent the reality you have created. So when you find the answers to question two of the Big Seven, even though it's an adaptation of a comic book, look for the reality, look for the truth.

The reader should be just as interested in the actions and motivations of the antagonist as he is in the actions and motivations of the protagonist. This means that our antagonist needs depth, he needs a story of his own, a story and background that not only motivate his actions but gives a certain credibility and twisted righteousness to his cause. This is the formula for the sympathetic villain. The antagonist does not have to be sympathetic (as we indicated in the *Harry Potter* chapter), but in the comic book world, they usually are. They've been wronged terribly in some way, and it's pushed them to where they are now. Comic villains need to be sympathetic because they recur. Oh, you might think they're dead, but they'll be back. If they are going to keep reappearing, they need to be interesting. And they may not necessarily be evil in the truest sense of the word. I hate to say it, but *deeply misguided* might describe them best.

You've started working on your comic book adaptation and you're clipping right along. You know who your main character is, and you know what he wants. So, we move on to the next step.

3. *Who/what keeps him from achieving what he wants (who/what are the apparent and true antagonists)?*

The first question here is the same question we had to answer regarding our main character. We have countless villains to pick from, so who do we choose and why? When you're working with a comic book adaptation, there's generally only one way to go for the first film. You have to use the primary antagonist, the archenemy if you will. Batman has the Joker, Superman has Lex Luthor, and the X-Men have Magneto. Not that it's brought to light in the film, but Sabertooth is also Wolverine's archenemy.

We've got that problem handled, but now, how do we use our antagonist? It's often more fun to create our villains (they get all the cool lines). We should, however, be careful in making our villains too sympathetic. They need to have a clear agenda and really be bad. In some films the antagonist actually overshadows the main character. Take *The Silence of the Lambs*, for example. It's all good and fine wondering what Clarice is going to do to catch Buffalo Bill, but what everyone really wants is to hear what that sick little monkey Hannibal Lecter is going to say next. (*Note:* the sequel wasn't called *Clarice*.) These stories are in the minority, but they teach us something that so many writers overlook. Every story is only as good as its antagonist. And even though we might be dealing with comic book characters here, that does not mean that these characters need to be paper-thin, one-dimensional caricatures.

Aside from being interesting and well developed, our antagonist should seem to be insurmountable. He's more powerful than the protagonist, smarter, more driven, ruthless, and uncompromising. This forces the main character to grow beyond what he is in order to defeat the villain. The antagonist provides the measurement of the width, breadth, depth, and execution of the main character's arc. The more diabolical the villain, the more the protagonist must endure in order to overcome him.

Magneto embodies all the qualities of the great antagonist. His cause is righteous but misguided. He is uncompromising. He's more powerful than the hero. He is intelligent, ruthless, and calculating, and we sympathize with his motives. The cadre of henchmen that follow him (Toad, Mystique, and Sabertooth) are well suited to the task of carrying out Magneto's plan. Back-story on these characters generally isn't necessary, at least not in the realm of the comic book adaptation. They serve as obstacles, stepping-stones to the primary antagonist. You must defeat his henchmen before you get to him.

We've established who the physical, apparent antagonists in this story are. But Logan has more to fight than the brotherhood of mutants. Logan's a loner, always has been, always will be. This is a trait, an instinct he must overcome if he wants to save Rogue and defeat Magneto. At the beginning of the story, Wolverine cares about no one but himself. We can never truly grow as human beings until we care about someone else more than we care about ourselves. Wolvie feels that it's best to stay out of other people's business, and he wants everyone else to stay out of his. Not only does he NOT want the responsibility of caring about someone else, he doesn't want the responsibility of some-one else caring about him. Then there are the shaded memories that haunt him in his sleep, the horrors of what happened to him fifteen years ago.

Our characters need internal conflict; without it, they are robots. In the end, no matter how interesting the story is, the characters are what the audience will remember. The more obstacles to conquer, the more interesting the arc.

4. *How in the end does he achieve what he wants in an unexpected, interesting, and unusual way?*

This means that Wolverine can't just slice and dice Magneto at the movie's climax. Sure, we kind of want him to, but what's unexpected and unusual about that? The story is set up in a way that will not allow this to happen. It prevents itself from being too predictable. Magneto can control metal, and Wolvie's body is full of adamantium. He can use Wolverine as a marionette. This goes back to the creation (or in the comic book case, the selection of) the primary antagonist. The hero must overcome everything that holds him back, both internally and externally. Then and only then can he succeed. We'll delve deeper into that matter when we reach question seven.

The most important thing to remember when we come to the climax is this: It's not the what, it's the how. It's okay if the reader knows what the ending will be. Of course, we realize that somehow Magneto will be defeated. The question is how the writer can make sure that it happens in an unexpected, interesting, and unusual way. But remember, Logan's goal is twofold: He must defeat Magneto and save Rogue.

Every time, that's the only way to do it: foreshadowing and payoff, BAM! If the events of the climax aren't foreshadowed, then they appear as nothing but coincidence, and you are not allowed any coincidences in the third act. We know what happens when Rogue touches another mutant, and we've seen what happened when she touched Wolverine. We suspect that this will play a role in the climax, but how it will happen, we can't be sure. When Wolverine does touch Rogue after he's destroyed Magneto's machine, nothing happens. Nice work. It's one last twist, one of the writer's final gifts to delight and thrill the audience. Although it's not particularly a convention of the comic book genre, it is a convention of good storytelling. When she does come to and take Wolverine's powers, I wouldn't say that we're surprised, but I wouldn't say that we anticipated the severity of the price Wolverine would pay, either.

Wolverine doesn't die, as we generally do not kill off our main characters, especially when we're dealing with this genre. Sequels are often the name of the game here. If they'll buy one, they'll buy two; if they'll buy two . . . and so on. While we want to tie up our loose ends, we also want to leave some teasers for a possible sequel. Not anything that would disrupt or discredit the original story, but small bread crumbs that we can follow into *X-Men II*.

5. *What are you trying to say by ending your story this way?*

This is a big question. Before we answer it, let's set down a rule. The message should come about as a result of the story. The story should not be a result of the message. What your story says in the end should be a reflection of your theme. In *X-Men*, you could say that as in *Shawshank*, "Hope springs eternal." Hope that history will not repeat itself, hope that humanity will come around, hope that Magneto will see he's only making humans more fearful of mutants, hope that if mutantkind follows the proper channels and fights for equality without resorting to terrorist tactics, that they will succeed in being treated fairly. The answer to all these questions at the end of the film is a resounding yes. There is hope, and maybe we all can live together, even though many of us are very different.

Think about your story and what its ending says. Is it a reflection of your theme? Be sure it's not too on the nose or too preachy. Odds are that most of the people who see a film couldn't tell you what the moral of the story is or what the film is saying. That's probably a good thing. If we get too far to the left or right of the spectrum, our story ends up becoming a result of the message. Everyone who saw X-Men won't be able to tell you what the film's ending meant. But they would know if it didn't mean anything or if it was too abstract, or most importantly, if it wasn't satisfying. If the ending works for them, whether they know it or not, they got the point. It's not at the surface of their consciousness, but they're aware on some level. How many times have you heard, "It was pretty good until the end"? In those cases, the writers didn't nail their endings, they did not reflect or justify their themes, and as a result, the audience was alienated.

6. *How do you want to tell your story (who should tell it, if anyone, and what narrative devices should you employ)?*

It's always a temptation for writers to use a narrator. That device frees us from so many of the burdens we face when composing a screenplay. We can just tell the audience what's going on and what already happened. We can say what people are thinking instead of finding a clever way for them to say what they're thinking. We can shed light on any subject without having to express it visually. In other words, we can shirk our responsibilities as storytellers and refuse to accept the full weight of the craft of screenwriting just to make our lives easier.

There are many different kinds of voice-over narration: voice-over as a setup or as a punch line, voice-over as inner thought, voice-over as an aside to the audience, voice-over as an explanatory device, and voice-over as a crutch for underdeveloped writing skills. That last one (in case you didn't catch it) is the bad kind. If the voice-over isn't adding to the story, it's detracting from it. Or worse yet, redundantly repeating it. Comic books are a visual medium akin to film in many ways. Both forms rely on pictures to tell the story. I love voice-over, but 99 percent of the time, the writer should try to express what would have been a voice-over as a more interesting and challenging visual. So unless you happen to be Frank Darabont or Stephen King, I encourage you to write your comic book adaptation in the third person with as little voice-over as possible.

I might be wrong, but I actually cannot think of any comic book adaptations that have used narrative voice-over, unless it's been to bookend the story. *X-Men* begins with a voice-over from Dr. Charles Xavier. It's short, it sets up the mutant phenomenon, and it's the last voice-over we hear for the rest of the film. From that point on, it's third person all the way.

Flashback is used in this story to good effect. The initial flashback shows us the origin of Magneto. The other shows us the origin of Rogue. This is important information on two of the principal characters. The key word there is *important*. If you're going to use flashback, make it short, make it sweet, and be sure that the information given reverberates throughout the rest of the story. Misused flashbacks are pus-filled lesions on the body of the story. If you use them, be sure you need them. In this kind of adaptation, they're used primarily to establish the origins of our heroes and villains.

Another device employed in *X-Men* is the dream sequence/ flashback. As you may have already guessed, these are flashbacks in the form of a dream. Do yourself a favor. When you use a dream sequence, please don't have your character "jolt from sleep" or "sit bolt upright." Every screenplay I read seems to end its dream sequences in this way. Granted, Wolverine awoke in this manner, but he also followed it up by slamming a trio of adamantium blades through Rogue's chest. There is a reason for him to wake up that way: so he can stab Rogue and she can take his powers, to foreshadow the events to come. Otherwise it would just be a cliché wake-up from a bad dream sequence.

When's the last time you sat straight up in bed from a nightmare anyway? I can't say that I ever have. In any case, try to find other ways for characters to wake up from bad dreams. You'll make the world a better place.

You've got lots of choices to make when you're deciding how to tell your story. Make sure that you're not choosing devices and tactics that exist solely to make it easier on you. If you decide to start your story at the middle, go back to the beginning, work your way back to the middle, then move forward to the end, and it's the biggest damn headache you've ever brought on yourself, before you trash this version, ask yourself one question: Does this structure make my story better? If the answer's yes, you know what to do.

7. *How do your main character and any supporting characters change over the course of the story?*

Not only does your main character have to change over the course of the story, but supporting characters need some manner of arc as well. Not all your supporting characters, but some. They have both internal and external battles to face, and this is what makes a memorable supporting cast. They don't have to climb the mountain our hero does, but at least give them some hills to traverse. Lois Lane is in love with Superman. She's a reporter and she knows the true identity of the Man of Steel. Love, or a career rocket ship to the top of the food chain? She chooses love. She wouldn't have chosen love initially, but that's her arc, her change. Let's examine the X-Men.

Scott Summers/Cyclops: Scott is the leader of the X-Men. He's a leader who's never really been tested, and he doubts his abilities on some level. Wolverine comes along and Scott sees someone who's more experienced, completely confident, and has the hots for his woman. By the time we've reached the climax, Scott is forced to take charge and lead his team. Something finally clicks and he steps into the leadership role with confidence and clarity. He even confirms this realization and newfound confidence verbally: "I have a shot. I'm taking it."

He has finally learned to make decisions and be confident in them.

Dr. Jean Grey: She also has a confidence problem regarding her abilities. She's almost afraid of her telepathic powers (not her telekinetic powers). She loves Scott, but Wolverine's putting the charm on her pretty heavy. She doesn't want to admit it, but she's a bit taken with him. Jean is forced to overcome her fear of her telepathy when she has to use Cerebro to find Rogue. Her telekinetic powers are also put to the test when she guides Wolverine to Magneto's machine atop the Statue of Liberty's torch as Storm flies him up in a whirlwind. After everything is said and done, Jean knows that she loves Scott and things would never work out between her and Logan. She even starts to tell Logan, but he cuts her off.

Marie/Rogue: Her power drove her from her home and isolated her from humanity and worse yet, from human touch. It's a terrible burden to bear, knowing that you'll never be able to touch another person without hurting them. She has to come to terms with her power if she's ever going to be happy again. After her near death at the hands of Magneto and her subsequent salvation due to Wolverine's sacrifice, she comes to realize that people care about her even if she's a mutant. They're not afraid of her any more, and she's not afraid of them.

Ororo Monroe/Storm: Storm did not have an arc, unless you count electrical arc.

Professor Charles Xavier: Xavier is a static character, for the most part. He believes the same things and holds the same values at the beginning of the film as he does at the end. But he is necessarily static. He is the unwavering mentor to the group. A man in charge needs to be solid and unwavering if his followers are to believe in him. His will is the rock upon which his organization stands or falls. He is to the X-Men what Magneto is to the brotherhood of Mutants.

Logan/Wolverine: Logan overcomes his loner instincts and works with the X-Men as a member of a team. He learns to care about someone else more than himself (Rogue). He puts his life on the line for her sake. In doing so, he reclaims a piece of his humanity he'd thought was lost. He's not necessarily a kinder, gentler Wolverine, but he's taking on the responsibility of caring about others and letting them care about him. He knows he doesn't have to do everything alone now. After years of keeping his nose out of other people's business and making sure they keep theirs out of his, he's finally chosen a side. He will fight the good fight. Even though much of humankind hates and fears him, he won't let that come in the way of protecting the innocent.

Pat yourself on the back, you made it through The Big Seven. You're pumped up and ready to start writing your comic book adaptation! Pull back the reins just a little bit longer lest your horse gallop uncontrolled into the desert. Instead, get him a drink of water and guide him gently into scene-o-gram country. I've filled in the boxes of this scene-o-gram with the specifics of the film *X-Men*. It may be useful to you as a guide when you fill out your own scene-o-gram. Which, of course, you are doing right now, frantically. Don't rush through it just to fill in the boxes, though. The more time you spend here, the easier it will be for you when you start setting your story to the page.

The Big Seven: *X-Men*

1. *Who is the main character?*
    Wolverine is the main character.

2. *What does Wolverine want/need/desire?*
    He wants to defeat Magneto and save Rogue. He wants to keep Rogue from becoming what he has become, and he wants to find out what happened to him fifteen years ago.

3. *Who/what keeps him from achieving what he wants?*

Wolvie is opposed by Magneto, his own unwillingness to be part of a team or have people care about him, and his "look-out-for-number-one" attitude.

4. *How in the end does Wolverine achieve what he wants in an unexpected, interesting, and unusual way?*

   Wolvie overcomes Magneto's evil threat by having Storm and Jean Grey catapult him to the top of the Statue of Liberty, whacking Magneto's machine, and letting Rogue take his powers.

5. *What are you trying to say by ending the story this way?*

   Ya gotta have faith, hope, and tolerance!!!

6. *How do you want to tell your story?*

   Chronologically, in the third person, with opening voice-over and limited flashbacks.

7. *How do your main character and any supporting characters change over the course of the story?*

   Wolverine learns to be part of a team and care about others more than himself. Cyclops learns that he has what it takes to be a leader. Rogue accepts what she is. Jean Grey gains confidence in her powers.

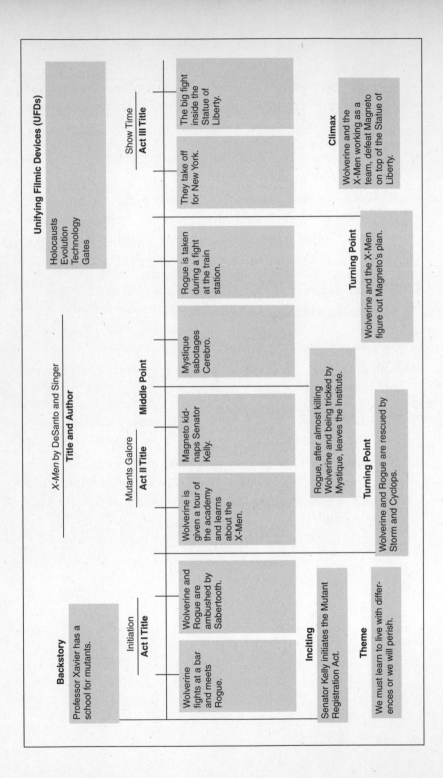

Unifying Filmic Devices (UFDs)

Holocausts
Evolution
Technology
Gates

X-Men by DeSanto and Singer
Title and Author

Backstory

Professor Xavier has a school for mutants.

Show Time
Act III Title

They take off for New York.

The big fight inside the Statue of Liberty.

Climax

Wolverine and the X-Men working as a team, defeat Magneto on top of the Statue of Liberty.

Mutants Galore
Act II Title

Middle Point

Wolverine is given a tour of the academy and learns about the X-Men.

Magneto kidnaps Senator Kelly.

Mystique sabotages Cerebro.

Rogue is taken during a fight at the train station.

Turning Point

Wolverine and the X-Men figure out Magneto's plan.

Rogue, after almost killing Wolverine and being tricked by Mystique, leaves the Institute.

Turning Point

Wolverine and Rogue are rescued by Storm and Cyclops.

Initiation
Act I Title

Wolverine fights at a bar and meets Rogue.

Wolverine and Rogue are ambushed by Sabertooth.

Inciting

Senator Kelly initiates the Mutant Registration Act.

Theme

We must learn to live with differences or we will perish.

12

Smart Choices with Source Material

Case Study: *Shiloh*

Works that fall in the young adult and children's categories present an interesting challenge to the would-be adaptor. The first choice that needs to be made is which way you're going to go with the adaptation. Some, such as *Harry Potter*, try to stay pretty faithful to the original, while others have taken the approach of a complete overhaul of the original work. This technique can work, but can also lead to heinous failures, such as a little film you may have had the misfortune of seeing called *Snow White: A Tale of Terror*. When the resulting adaptation of the source material has a completely different tone, there is great potential for trouble. For example, there's a video game out right now called *Alice*. It's a rather horrific take on *Alice in Wonderland*, and is currently being adapted for the screen. How's that for adaptation? A book adapted to a video game adapted to a screenplay. One wonders, why even bother adapting something if you are going to completely alter and revise it anyway?

Okay, so there's my take on complete revisionism, and that's one way to go with your adaptation of this genre. Sadly, or in some cases not so sadly, most of these adaptations end up going straight to video or tanking in the theater. There's gotta be a good one sooner or later, though. What gets in the way of these adaptations is the fact that tonally, the source material itself is completely different. It would be much like adapting *Friday the 13th* into a delightful children's novel. I don't know about you, but I don't want to see Jason Vorhees having an epiphany while pushing the merry-go-round at the local preschool!

Adaptation is more often about making smart choices than it is about making radical ones. The measure of the adaptor is how well he or she can use the source material, not how well he or she can maim it. There is, of course, a time and place for completely turning the source material on its head—just look at how well *O Brother, Where Art Thou?* played with *The Odyssey* and yet still did not betray its essence. Step back for a second and think about it. If you are adapting popular source material, give a little credit to the original. It was popular for a reason. And so, yes, you can alter it any way you need to, but don't lose the essence that drew you to the material in the first place.

If adaptation, then, is clearly about choices, let us look at some of the choices writer/director Dale Rosenbloom had to make when adapting Phyllis Naylor's Newberry Award–winning novel *Shiloh*. The novel is written in a beautifull, powerful voice; it is a fine example of a first-person narrative. The simplest way to translate this interior voice is through a voice-over narrative. Many writers would go this route, but in lieu of having voice-over, Rosenbloom chose to relate the tale from the third person, concentrating on the main character, Marty.

Much of the book is spent with Marty and his dog, Shiloh, or with Marty completely alone. This works great in a novel, but in a screenplay our characters need someone to interact with. Rosenbloom needed a device for Marty to articulate all that he was thinking and feeling. Thus, in the film we find the introduction of Marty's friend Samantha, a character completely unique to the screenplay. She allows Marty to now have an audience surrogate, if you will, who serves the same purpose as the interior monologues in the book. Samantha is someone Marty could talk to, bounce ideas off of, a co-conspirator. Doc Wallace (who was originally Doc Murphy in the novel) is also someone else Marty can talk to. Though he wasn't that pivotal of a figure in the novel, Rosenbloom uses him as a moral and ethical mentor for Marty.

There are also some things in the book that would have garnered a PG-13 rating had they been kept in the screenplay. Originally Marty finds Judd right after he's shot a deer out of season. He strikes a deal to work for Judd in exchange for keeping quiet, and together the two drag the carcass back to Judd's. Then they try to hide the blood and cover the drag trail. You can't very well have people dragging around dead deer in a children's film, though. Rosenbloom opted to use a rabbit. Judd didn't kill the rabbit, either. Same effect, a lot less blood. In the novel, there's a lot of talk (in Marty's head) about a dog that he found close to Judd's house with a bullet hole in its head. In the film, it's only mentioned once. If you're making a movie geared for children, you can't cross over the PG-13 line. (Apparently there's some biochemical reaction that takes place at age thirteen that makes them capable of handling more adult material.)

There are many other changes as well in Rosenbloom's adaptation. For instance, Marty's mother selling homemade nail polish is something new to the film. It gives her a little time in the spotlight and a little more depth. One of the biggest changes from book to the film is the ending. The way in which Marty wins Shiloh from Judd differs significantly in the screenplay. In the novel, Marty gradually wins Judd's respect as he works for him and as a result, Judd lets him keep the dog. That's all well and good, and it plays out wonderfully in the novel. However, it's not exactly what you'd call a big climax for a film.

So Rosenbloom had to invent a new scene that wasn't in the novel. Rosenbloom's answer was to have a scene in which Judd comes to Marty's house to take the dog from him, and we get a big final confrontation. Marty still gets the dog, of course, only in a different way. This is a wonderful example of how important it is not to bind yourself to the original material. It seems that the best way to honor the original work is to remain as close tonally as you can while adding or subtracting what you need to make the movie work. *Shiloh* has done this admirably.

Writer, director, and producer Dale Rosenbloom was gracious enough to agree to talk with me about the process he went through in adapting this beautifully written novel into an equally beautifully executed film, which he also directed. *Shiloh* won the 1997 Genesis Award for Best Feature Film as well as numerous other distinctions, including top honors at the Chicago International Children's Film

Festival, the Heartland Film Festival, and a Gold Medal Special Jury Prize at the Charleston Film Festival. Dale is a USC film school graduate who has also written *Shiloh 2: Shiloh Season*, *Shiloh 3*, and *Instant Karma*. He has produced *Reckless Indifference*, *Eight Days a Week*, *Red Ribbon Blues*, *Ride with the Wind*, *A Woman, Her Men and Her Futon*, and *Across the Tracks*.

Instead of going though another analysis of how the Big Seven have been addressed in this adaptation, I thought it would be more fun to read an interview in which writer/director Rosenbloom talks about his personal process and the real-life journey he went through in writing this adaptation, getting it made, and getting it onto the big screen. Enjoy!

An Interview with Dale Rosenbloom

Q: *You told me that a lot of people said* Shiloh *couldn't be made into a movie.*

A: Yes, that was the feeling because so much of the book—the whole book—is told from an internal lead character point of view. So how do you get these feelings and thoughts across? Marty's talking to himself, he's inside his own head. What can you do to convey that to an audience? That was viewed as a very difficult thing to do.

Q: *Were these studio executives who told you this?*

A: When I read the book, it had not gotten awards and all of that and it had been shopped to all the studios. So yes, that's what they said, but still, I think a lot of people liked it because it's a wonderful book. But nobody was saying they wanted to make it into a movie. They also said it was a genre whose time had come and gone.

Q: *What year are we talking about?*

A: This was 1992. Then, while we were discussing the option again, the book won the Newbery Medal.

Q: *Let me take you back for a second. How would you go about contacting an author to option material? How did you do that? What's your advice?*

A: Find out who the publisher is, generally. Contact them. Back then it was fairly easy. The publisher would put you in contact with the agent. But it's changed a lot, since so many more books are now being optioned for film and television. So what happens now is a publisher generally wants you to e-mail or fax them and they'll respond to you. Sometimes they take a month or two, sometimes they do it right away. You try and find out who that author's representative is or who their agent is. Sometimes it's the publishers themselves. Like Scholastic Books, for example. They handle the film rights for a lot of their authors. I think they're signed with AMG to handle their movie rights. But there're some Scholastic authors that have their own representation.

In the case of *Shiloh*, I read the book—I think I gave it to my nephews, too. I said to myself, "I'm sorry, but I really think there's a movie here." I talked to a few people. They said, "Oh, it's a family movie, it's hard to get those made." All that sort of stuff. I went about optioning it. Found out who the publisher and who the rep were. It actually turned out that the guy representing the book was an agent at my own agency. Which didn't make the negotiation any easier, but it still was a good entrée. So we made overtures to option the book and then when it came time for them to say okay or not on the deal, right at the very moment, it wins the Newbery Medal. They were very dignified about the whole thing, though. They won this big award, and my fear was that they were going to break the deal and try to sell it now. But they didn't. We ended up making a deal and shopped the book.

Q: *Without a screenplay?*

A: Without a screenplay, without a director, without anything. We thought, "It won the Newbery Medal, it's great, it's going to be a children's classic, let's go out with a book." We went to a bunch of places and a few places actually were interested. But once it got to a level where they were potentially going to put up money, they all passed. Disney actually came very close to optioning the book from me. They ultimately passed, saying that they felt the adaptation was too hard to do. I talked to my agent about it and said, "Hey, why don't I just write a script for it."

So I went off and did the adaptation. Which was a challenge. It was something I had never done before. But it was great source material. I really felt the story was there. Then I had a script.

Q: *Let's talk about that. You did make some very specific changes; you had to. Can you talk about some of the choices you made? For example, why you introduced the little girl Samantha?*

A: Early on, we knew we needed a sounding board for Marty. We went back and forth: Should he talk to his parents, should he talk to one of his sisters, what about Doc Wallace? This was a movie, not a book, so I felt we needed another location. I felt we were really lacking—as it is, there's still not a lot of locations in the movie. The feeling was that we needed to expand it, to make it a little bit bigger. I also felt we needed other characters to have a relationship with Marty and to comment on Judd and the family relationships. So Doc Wallace and his wife became the characters with the general store. The feeling was that if Doc could be a character that's kind of a paternal figure to Marty, that's another character that's a sounding board for him, and an advisor. So much of the drama has to do with lying to his family and what that means. Is that kind of dishonesty justified because it potentially saves Shiloh's life? He struggles with all these things.

The character Samantha was created to be the sounding board for all the stuff that builds up in the beginning of the movie, to show where Marty's at, to show that he's lonely, to show that he really doesn't have a lot to do. He wants a bike, but he has to save for a bike. It also shows how his priorities change. Instead of going to work to get the bike, he goes to work to buy Shiloh. Which, of course, doesn't necessarily work when Judd changes the deal. The theory was that Samantha would be that person who formally was his internal dialogue. She gave more life to Marty on the screen, life that he wouldn't have had if he was isolated. She has a crush on Marty and is dealing with preadolescence. Marty kind of likes her, too.

Q: *During the adaptation process, how much dialogue from the book did you keep and how much did you create?*

A: There was some great dialogue. There's a lot of dialogue from the book in the script. A lot of it's been pared down, a lot of it's been transferred from one scene to another, and a lot of it is original dialogue. When I first sent the author the draft, she wasn't that happy with it. I decided early on that I wanted to have a good relationship with her. I really liked her, I had a great respect for her as a writer and a real respect for her as a person. I felt that it wouldn't be fair to just invite her to a screening or send her a tape and say, "What do you think?"

Q: *But contractually, you had every right to do anything you wanted, whether she was happy with it or not.*

A: Yeah, we could have done anything. We sent her a draft of the script and even though so much of the dialogue was similar, she didn't quite know about the character Samantha. She wondered what happened to Doc Murphy. Why he was Doc Wallace and why he suddenly had a general store. I'd changed the dynamic a lot. Shiloh becomes more of a character in the movie than in the book. That's probably because it's visual, you can see the dog. I know that she wasn't thrilled with it.

One thing in particular that we'd struggled with was the ending. In the book, after reneging on the deal, Judd essentially gives in. Marty tells him he needs to do the right thing and honor the deal and all that sort of stuff. On the page, it's very dramatic and emotional. It's a great ending. Onscreen, it just wouldn't work.

So I wrote this courtroom scene where Judd calls the cops to come and get Shiloh because it's his property. The police have no choice but to take the dog. There's a hearing the next day. Shiloh's in a holding cell, all alone for that night. Judd and Marty plead their cases, and Judd is awarded Shiloh. Although the judge chastises him and tells him what he really thinks of him. Marty has that line in the movie, "All I had was your word, ain't that worth something to you?"

Judd changes his mind in that setting and gives Marty the dog. Phyllis hated it. I was never ecstatic about it either, but it was a way to make it more dramatic. She said, "It was the hand of God coming in. How could we do that?"

I understood what she was saying, although I felt it was a very dramatic scene. We just kept going back and forth, back and forth. Actually, I think we went out with the courtroom draft when we were casting because we didn't have an alternative ending. I went back to the book asking how we could make the ending one step beyond what it was. To make it more dramatic. In the book, just as the deal between Marty and Judd ends, Marty gets Shiloh as promised, but in the script, I wanted Judd to change his mind and Marty is denied. This would allow us to carry it another step, to carry it to another sequence.

So Marty goes home, Judd's reneged on the deal, he's not gonna let Shiloh go no matter what. Judd comes to the house now and physically threatens Marty. It gets to the point where Judd takes the dog, puts him in the truck, and drives away. At that moment, when he looks in the rearview mirror, he sees Marty with his father. Who knows what's going on in his brain? But he has a moment of sobriety. That one sober moment where he realizes that the dog has a name now—the dog loves the kid, the kid loves the dog. The dog's useless to him anyway, as far as he's concerned. This one time he's gonna do something right. He's going to do the honorable thing. He opens the door and lets the dog out.

It ended up working, visually. In the editing room, we had this inspiration that the scene was playing too fast. I thought, why don't we have Shiloh thinking about his life with Marty? Mark Westmore, the editor, played with it. He did these "Shiloh memories," very briefly. It ended up working because it brings everybody back to where Shiloh's been and what he's losing, especially the boy's friendship. That helps the ending work.

If you read the script, even the shooting script, even as we made the movie, the end doesn't have the same impact as when you have an actor like Scott Wilson playing Judd. You can see in his eyes and there's so much more there than you put on the page. You see the dog and the flashbacks and they carry a much greater resonance than anything you can write in a screenplay.

Q: *Let's go back a bit. You have a draft of a script that everyone likes. What did you do next?*

A: My agent sent it out to about ten or twelve places, producers. It got a great response. Out of the ten producers, five wanted to take it to a studio. At the studio level, two or three places were really interested. We actually had offers, MGM, I think. We had an offer from MPCA, which was making a lot of movies at the time. There was another offer from Disney, for the Disney Channel, that was very interesting.

The problem was, by that time I was in year three of my option. I had already spent what for me was a pretty sizable amount of money on the option. I'd written the script, and the amount of money that they were willing to pay for an option would barely cover my option costs. They weren't much interested in me directing it. It was a development deal, and I wasn't too excited about any of that. If any of these deals that weren't offering a lot of money had at least said that they really intended to make the movie, then that would have been more interesting.

A lot of times people develop things because they need a certain type of movie, or someone in the company happens to like the script. That doesn't necessarily mean that they're willing to spend the millions of dollars it takes to make a movie. Rather than jumping onto those offers, we pulled back to find another way to get it made. I started thinking about trying some of the independents. That's where we went for the next step. We passed on the offers we had and looked to do it independently.

Q: *What was the budget of the film you ended up making?*

A: The budget, I can't exactly reveal that, but it was in the low millions.

Q: *Did you go out and try to raise the money yourself?*

A: We went out and—at the time it was 1995—there was an emergence of a bigger foreign market. Though this movie didn't have huge presale value overseas, there was still a value to it. We got a bank and our attorney and did minimum estimates, and through some borrowing and some private investors, we managed to put together a budget. While we were shooting the movie, it was looking pretty good. We decided to finish it at Technicolor and do it in Dolby Digital, which ended up costing us plenty, but our investors ended up doing very nicely.

We had a situation after we finished the film, where we didn't really have any offers. We'd won all these film festivals and all the critics liked it, but no one was interested, with the exception of Disney Channel. There were some people associated with the project that thought, "Hey, great, you made it to the Disney Channel." But there were others, myself included, that just didn't want it to be a Disney Channel movie. There's nothing wrong with Disney Channel movies, but I really felt that we had something more.

So we went everywhere. We heard the same thing from every place: wonderful movie, we really think people would enjoy it a lot, but in order to make it a theatrical release—this little movie which most people thought was a six-to-eight million-dollar flick—we need to spend about fifteen million dollars on prints and advertising. They didn't feel they could justify that.

Disney looked at it as a feature. We talked to the president of Disney, Joe Roth. He was highly complimentary. He liked the movie a lot. But basically, he said he couldn't justify spending fifteen million in P&A; the numbers just don't pan out. Universal was another place, we screened it for them four times. Finally, they said they just couldn't justify the spending. Warner Brothers, too. Everybody passed. We were kind of stuck and kept doing the festival thing. By that time, several critics had said it was one of the best family films in many years.

An executive at New Line, a guy named Mitch Goldman, was president of marketing and distribution; he was really interested in buying the film. But he had the same problem everyone else had: "How do I get this movie out without spending money all over the place?" I guess he couldn't get the support from the people at New Line. To be honest, I don't know what happened. But we asked him what we should do with it. We didn't know if we should go back to Disney Channel. He said, "No, you can't do that."

"Then what do we do?"

He said he knew someone that might be able to help us. Someone who would do something unusual. So he introduced us to this guy who I'd actually met before, through Mitch, but only casually, Seth Willenson.

Seth was kind of a legendary guy. He was a brilliant strategizer and marketing/distribution guy. I called Carl Borack, one of the producers of *Shiloh*, and asked him to send Seth a tape. He refused to send him one. He wanted Seth to see the movie onscreen. That's one thing that's a very valuable lesson. If you ever have the opportunity to screen a movie for somebody, do everything you can to actually screen the movie—unless it looks bad on film. It makes such a big difference, and you know someone's going to watch it all the way through. What happens with tapes is that people put them in and if the first five or fifteen minutes aren't fast-paced enough they move on to the next one. It's hard to get a fair shot.

Anyway, Carl and Seth go back and forth and eventually we paid for the screening. We screen *Shiloh* for him and he's in love with the movie. He said it was an easy sale. Yeah, right. He asked where we'd been. We told him the people we had been to see and he said we were going to the wrong division. We needed to go to the video division. We said we didn't want it to be just a video. He said the video division would pay for the theatrical, this was going to be a huge video. He saw it, he knew that there was something there. We ended up with three places interested.

Seth actually advised us to take the deal that wasn't necessarily the best up-front deal, but it allowed us to retain ownership of the movie. That was with Warner Brothers. We went with them and they were very enthusiastic about the movie. The plan for the release was in 1997 and the movie was completed in mid-1996. Now it was the end of 1996 and Warner Brothers wanted it on their slate for spring of 1997.

They allowed us an eight-week window for theatrical release. The movie came out at the end of April, then it came out on tape at the end of June. We're prepped for that release. And at the time, there were about thirty-five or forty small theatrical releases and/or straight-to-video releases every year. So it was a small market, relative to today—we're talking about two or three a month, maybe four a month. *Shiloh* found its niche there. We hit the market at the right time.

Since then, the market has changed a lot. Right now, there are 110 to 120 straight-to-video or limited theatrical releases that go straight to video every year. Disney decided to get into that business. One of the things that also happened is people tried to duplicate what they called "the *Shiloh* model." Which was do a limited theatrical release, and then let the theatrical serve as marketing for the video. Let the theatrical perform or not perform. If it makes money or doesn't make money, it's justified. It's an awareness that the movie isn't just a straight-to-video movie.

But with *Shiloh*, people ended up actually wanting to see the movie in the theater. To such an extent that—it became so popular in that limited time—it was never in more than a dozen or so cities at a time because there were never more than sixty or so prints made. What they would do was move from city to city and the film did enormously well during the weekend matinee times. There was really nothing else out there. At any given moment, there are only one or two family films in the theaters, that's it. If you want to find more movies for ten and unders, it's really hard to do. It's something I've always felt studios are missing the boat on.

We performed well enough theatrically that the movie played in about thirty-nine cities, grossing a million something dollars. Which was great. We were only expecting around half a million. The movie kept playing a couple months after the video had come out in stores. I've always found that strange but wonderful that people would still go to the movie even though they could get it on video. That's what happened.

Q: *Any advice for aspiring writers doing their own adaptations?*

A: I would tell you this: It's been my experience that people who have the power to greenlight projects in Hollywood like to have an element attached. It could be a movie star, a big director, a big producer, or a lot of money coming into the project. Financing, a distribution partner, any number of those types of things. But also, it could be a book or TV property. Something where there's a real name recognition of the preexisting property. It gives credibility. When you have a book that you've optioned, that's been published and, hopefully, sold well, or praised, or it's just really good.

Whoever's making the decisions to move forward, has the ability to say no. Someone else already decided that it was good enough to give the go-ahead in another form. It was a hit book, or a book that got published. There's a psychological comfort level for that executive who wants to go to the next step. It's harder to say no in that case. It's easy to say no to a script, they get hundreds of those. But if you have a book, they think, "Heck, Simon and Schuster published it, so there must be something to the story." The worst you can say is that it's more of a book than a movie. There is, I think, a definite advantage. I think it's up to about 40 percent of all movies are adaptations. That says something. You've got an in that you don't have with an original screenplay.

Q: *What about the physical process? Any advice on tackling the writing of it?*

A: It depends on what your source material is. I've had experience with some sci-fi books that if we did them as straight adaptations, they wouldn't work on the screen. Some don't work because there's too much information or there's not enough information or they don't have enough story or they have too much story.

There might be too many characters or too much going on. It all depends.

My advice is to find something that you're passionate about, something that you've fallen in love with. An adaptation that you can relate to for whatever personal reason, whatever it is about it that touches you. Even if it's just that you always loved this type of movie or book, even if it's a thriller or sci-fi book that has no direct correlation to your life. At least be the person that sees something unique in it and be the one to adapt it. Find the story and find the characters. I don't think that a page—*Harry Potter* notwithstanding—I don't think a page-for-page, scene-for-scene adaptation generally works. I don't think it does a service to the moviegoing audience; it doesn't do a service to the book-reading audience.

Obviously, no matter what, there are some people you just can't win with. People who want you to adapt the book just as it was written. Then there will be people who say that you didn't change it enough. You just have to do what feels right. Remember that film is visual. Don't get stuck in a place where you have to have every detail. Lengthy descriptions don't matter in a script; throw them out. The characters' actions, their dialogue, the scenes have to portray the text. There's nothing worse than reading a heavy text script with all this information that you cannot convey on the screen.

Make sure that what you're saying in the script can be shown. Don't go into: "Rich was a great guy when he was a kid and he did this or that. Then, when he got older, he had his heart broken, but still managed to find love."

It doesn't do anything if you can't show it. "As he pulled the gun out, he was thinking about how his mother didn't give him corn flakes in the morning." This kind of stuff ends up in scripts I read and people try to say that it's important to subtext and character or backstory. I don't agree. Don't overwrite.

I've recommended adaptation to a lot of people. If you find the right piece of material it only helps—it doesn't guarantee you anything—but it only helps get you in. Look, if Julia Roberts is attached to your original screenplay, it's a lot better than having a book that is successful. Short of having someone that gets you to that next level, it really does help to have a book that you can say was translated into twelve languages or sold 300,000 copies. Suddenly they think that you're someone they should talk to. It will help you get yourself an agent, all that kind of stuff. Adaptations are a good way to go.

The Big Seven: *Shiloh*

1. *Who is your main character?*
   Marty Preston.

2. *What does Marty want/need/desire?*
   Marty wants to save Shiloh.

3. *Who/what keeps him from achieving what he wants?*
   His parents, his poverty, and most significantly, Judd Travers.

4. *How in the end does Marty achieve what he wants in an unexpected, interesting, and unusual way?*
   By winning over Judd with hard work and love.

5. *What are you trying to say by ending the story this way?*
   Ya gotta be honest and work hard!!! And don't forget to not judge people just by the way they look.

6. *How do you want to tell your story?*
   Chronologically, in the third person, with Marty as protagonist.

7. *How do your main character and any supporting characters change over the course of the story?*
   Marty learns the importance of honesty and hard work. Judd learns to love a little. Marty's mother learns to speak up for herself.

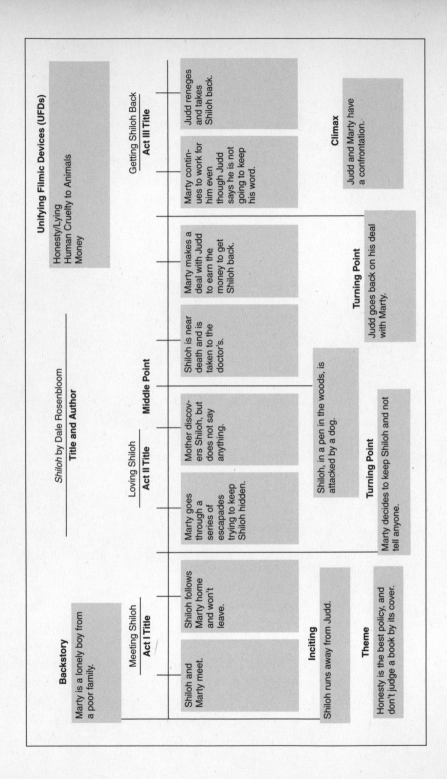

13

Hints from and Interviews with Hollywood Bigwigs

Now that you've read about my five-step adaptation process and seen it applied to all different types of genres, I would like to conclude with hints, tips, and quotes from screenwriters who specialize in adaptations, as well as other assorted Hollywood bigwigs.

First of all, I had the rare privilege of interviewing Emmy, WGA and Humanitas Award winning television writer Larry Brody, who has authored over 500 different television episodes and movies of the week. He has produced shows including *Star Trek*, *Diagnosis Murder*, *Walker, Texas Ranger*, *The Streets of San Francisco*, *Barretta*, *Police Story*, *Gibbsville*, *Spawn*, and *Silver Surfer*. He can be reached at his website, TVWriter.com.

"My first experience with writing an adaptation was when I worked on a series called *Gibbsville* in the early seventies. The series was based on practically every short story written by John O'Hara in the forties and fifties. I was young and just starting out, but they made me executive story consultant of the series, which meant that I either wrote or rewrote every script, under the supervision of the producer, John Furia, one of the great old pros of the TV business. O'Hara wrote wonderful dialogue, but he didn't write scenes per se. He told a story in the standard literary form, stringing it out length-wise. Film and television are written in scenes. Small, discreet pieces with a beginning, middle, and end. With a build to a punch of some kind that keeps the viewer watching for the next scene. What this means is that none of O'Hara's dialogue worked within the context of our form of drama. It didn't work within the realm of genuine human contact. And that's what you get in film and TV . . . human contact. Real actors standing there and automatically creating the expectation that they're going to communicate, act, and react, the way real human beings do.

"What I saw while working on this script, and then on all the others, was that when a novelist or short story writer writes dialogue he uses it to advance the story. People come right out and tell each other what's going on. Or they hide what's going on from each other but tell the reader because the reader is privy to the characters' innermost thoughts. When you're writing a script, though, all the audience gets are the words and the movement and the actors' eyes. The scriptwriter has to figure out how to say—without saying—certain things that a person wouldn't really say but would hide. To do that you have to add scenes and activities that didn't happen in the original work but which illustrate what the language used by the original writer actually said.

"With John O'Hara, who had this beautiful simplicity of language in narration as well as dialogue, we had to find a way to translate his style into a visual tool so that the viewer would get the same effect the reader got. Verbal style had to become visual style. That meant probing past the actual language to the writer's intentions, to the feelings and thoughts he wanted to convey, and conveying them in a filmic way.

"More than twenty years later, I was lured out of retirement to do two more adaptations for television, both comic books: *The Silver Surfer* and *Spawn*. I had been a huge comics fan. Fox had a deal to bring the Marvel comic *The Silver Surfer* to TV as a Saturday morning animation series. I was thrilled to be adapting one of my favorite comic books for TV. After watching some Saturday morning shows, though, I was disillusioned. How could I write that childish *biff-bam-boom* crap? Especially since the comic itself had been very adult, perhaps the most adult-oriented of all the Marvel comics?

"I met with the executive in charge and he swore up, down, and sideways that we would be doing the show for adults but showing it in a kids' time slot. The idea was to be as true as possible to what the comic had been, which was for the most part a highly philosophical work. Essentially, the Silver Surfer is Jesus Christ. Galactus, who is for all practical purposes God in terms of his power, has exiled the Surfer from the rest of the universe, cast him down, banished him, trapped him on Earth. Here on Earth, the Surfer doesn't understand anything men do. He thinks they're foolish and wrongheaded. In its first incarnation, the comic in fact failed because it was taken up in large part by Hamletlike soliloquies where the Surfer mused about why humans were so hard on each other, and 'How can I help them and not have to hurt them with my "power cosmic?"' He would agonize along these lines for fifteen pages and then zap the crud out of the bad guys for the last five. It was fascinating stuff. Very experimental for its time . . . and very experimental for Fox Kids.

"In television, writers and producers have many masters. I had to make the head of Marvel comics happy. I had to make the heads of Saban Productions, which was putting out most of the money and doing all the artwork and production, happy. I had to make the head of the toy company that was going to base an entire line of toys on the series happy. And I had to make Stan Lee, who was the cocreator of the Silver Surfer—with the late Jack Kirby—happy as well, because he was not only a legendary comics writer whose work I had devoured many years ago, he was still the official publisher of Marvel and executive producer of the show. And I also had to make myself happy as well—by doing a Silver Surfer that the Surfer would approve of if the Surfer was real.

"In Saturday morning animation, the definition of a good script is one that has three lines of dialogue and three pages of fighting per scene. It's 'talk, talk, talk,' and then, 'fight, fight, fight, fight, fight, fight . . .' and on and on. Saturday morning is done in sixty-five-episode blocks that can be shown weekly for two and a half years and then 'stripped' daily forever afterward for an audience that's about six years old. That's the only kind of show Saban understood. The only kind that the current group that ran Marvel understood. Ditto the toy company. And, surprisingly to me, the same for Stan Lee. Stan shocked me because he didn't seem to know the character nearly as well as I did. He was the first one to suggest that we play down the Surfer's nonviolent attitude and tendency toward introspection.

"TV animation was filled with shows about superheroes operating on Earth, so I wanted to put the Surfer back in space. I wanted the Surfer's plight to be the same as Ulyssis". He's trying to get home to the woman he loves, but he can't, because Galactus has moved the planet to an unknown region of space and the Surfer literally can't find it.

"Everyone involved bought into that immediately because it gave us a chance for more action without having to resort to fight after fight—I mean, surfing through space on cosmic waves, now that's action, right? And yet it kept the original feeling of the character. And how can you argue with *The Odyssey*? My version of the Silver Surfer then became the story of Ulysses if he was Jesus, on a never-ending quest to find his home. He comes close, but always fails. He succeeds at helping others, but always at the expense of attaining his own goals. Marvel had become big because of the bittersweet endings in many of its comic stories. I made all the Surfer endings bittersweet. As a hero, he won because he saved someone else, but as a man he always lost because he sacrificed his quest.

"Even though everyone was on the same page, I still had some problems regarding the actual writing of the scripts. The rest of the 'team' was always pressuring me for fewer speeches, shorter speeches, even shorter words. They also wanted still more visuals, 'eye candy,' and then the Standards and Practices Department at Fox Kids—the censors who make sure the network doesn't get complaints about being a bad influence on kids—stepped in and said we had to soft-pedal the Jesus thing . . . and that we could never in any context, in any show, any publicity, or any personal appearance, even mention the biblical aspect.

"I wanted to do something similar on *Spawn*, but there I had the opposite pressure. Todd MacFarlane was a very active executive producer with a very definite idea of who his character was, what he could do, and what his audience wanted. He had created a difficult character—a demon who when he was human was a hit man for the CIA, but whose personality was totally passive, who never acted but was only acted upon. In a sense, Spawn was more like the original comic book Silver Surfer than my television Surfer. He even had a similar overall problem. After the man who became Spawn was killed, he made a deal with the devil to go back to our plane of existence. He did it because he had a wife and daughter he loved, and whom he wanted to be with. But when he's returned here Spawn discovers that he's now a hideous monster who can never show himself to those he wants to be with.

"Todd was very anti-dialogue. He wanted to tell everything visually. So with Spawn I wrote to his specifications, meaning that I set up situations where Spawn would be victimized and finally be forced to take action to save himself from losing even the ugly little life he now had. He very seldom spoke, but because of the great art director, and Todd's constant pressure on the animators and artists, Spawn's face became as expressive as that of the best live actor, a very unusual situation in TV animation.

"For *Spawn*, the stories were all new, based on a six-episode arc I devised that would bring increased self-awareness to a character who begins as an almost mindless monster and then discovers who and what he really is, all, as I say, shown visually with startlingly good— and shocking—graphics on a much higher order than Fox Kids could afford. For *The Silver Surfer*, Marvel gave me every comic that the Surfer had ever appeared in, and our original plan was to adapt the plots of the comics whenever possible. I soon saw, though, that the plots weren't very good, which goes a long way toward explaining why the Surfer has come and gone throughout the years in comics instead of being a steady seller. The original Surfer was so busy philosophizing that he never did anything. We ended up using the plot of one comic, a graphic novel in which the Surfer comes home and everything goes wrong. The woman he loves even dies. Sidney loved the irony inherent in this concept, so we set up a story arc that would lead to that moment in the second thirteen episodes of the series.

"For the first thirteen *Surfer* episodes, we used a villain familiar to Surfer fans as his main nemesis and then had individual episodes involving other Marvel characters who lived in space and their various crises, leading up to the Surfer having to save the entire universe from being destroyed by that main nemesis, whose name was Thanos. In episode thirteen, in fact, the Surfer fails and all is lost! Then we wrote the next thirteen, in which the Surfer is able to recreate the universe. The first thing he does in 'his' universe is find his hidden home planet and his true love, Shalla Bal. But a terrible tragedy occurs and she seems to die. This drives the Surfer insane because by being able to create the universe he has, in his own mind, become a kind of God, and now God has been bested. Determined to make the universe a better place, the Surfer goes off to enforce his ethics and morality on all living creatures, for what he believes is their own good. This leads to all kinds of undesirable consequences, as in effect the Surfer becomes the ultimate villain, imposing his will on others.

"I had written or co-written all of the first thirteen scripts and did the same with this next group, but they were never produced. Not because no one liked them. On the contrary, everyone loved this approach. Primarily, I think, because it meant we could have more fights involving the Surfer. Instead, the problem was purely a business one. Marvel went bankrupt and couldn't pay its percentage of the production costs for the series, so Saban refused to produce any episodes beyond the first thirteen. Since we had destroyed the universe in episode thirteen and revived it in fourteen, in the 'real' world of television it stayed destroyed. On *Spawn*, which was scheduled so that only adults could see it, this would not only have been excusable, it would've been a big plus.

"The way I see it, the key to adapting literary material from any print medium is to be really familiar with that material. You have to know it backward and forward and sideways. It has to become part of you, as though it's your original creation.

"The most important thing you can do is know exactly what effect the original has on the reader and understand why it has that effect. Normally you're adapting material because it's already proven itself to be successful. Well, there's a reason it's a hit. There's a reason you want to make a film or a TV show or a kids' series out of it. That reason is the effect the book had on you. Your mission in this situation is to determine exactly why it affected you as it did and then duplicate that in any way you can. Going to the heart and soul of the original and bringing them to your new medium is, I think, the key to successful adaptation.

"It is not about duplication. That would be a disservice to the original, to the audience, and to yourself as a creative artist. Film doesn't work for the same reason that print works. Screenwriters don't naturally express themselves the way print writers do. It's not a matter of adapting word by word. It's digging out what feelings the work created in you and then working like hell to create those same feelings in a new generation that's going to see this great story or novel or comic or character instead of read him. Our job as adaptors is to use the values inherent in our medium to breathe new life into a work that we love and want to enable others to love."

Michael Hauge, author of *Writing Screenplays That Sell*, is a screenwriting coach and teacher who consults with Hollywood writers, directors, and production companies. He is also the creator of the website ScreenplayMastery.com.

"All filmmaking, and all storytelling, has one primary objective: to elicit emotion in the audience. This objective is achieved with only three basic elements, which form the foundation of all story: *character, desire,* and *conflict.*

"The basis of all good myths, legends, epic poems, fairy tales, plays, operas, short stories, true stories, novels, screenplays, TV episodes, movies, and Harry Chapin songs is simply this: *Emotionally involving characters must overcome seemingly insurmountable obstacles in order to achieve their compelling desires.* This single sentence must therefore form the foundation of any screenplay you hope to sell to Hollywood.

"Because screenplays and movies are so much more narrowly defined than any of those other forms of fiction, anyone adapting an existing story into film must abide by strict rules of character, desire, and conflict. In a movie, the character must be a hero or protagonist with whom we empathize, who is pursuing a *visible* goal with a clearly defined end point, and who must face terrifying obstacles created by other characters or forces of nature.

"This visible goal—what I term *outer motivation* in my book and seminars—must have a clearly defined endpoint or finish line. It defines the *story concept* or logline of the film, it will give the audience a clear idea of exactly what they're rooting for the hero(es) to achieve, and it tells us exactly what will represent success for the hero at the end of the film.

"This is the challenge if you're writing an adaptation: No other story form has these same requirements. Novels, plays, and true stories, for example, can follow multiple characters through long expanses of time as they pursue a series of desires. Their goals can be interior—a desire for acceptance, for example, or to resolve some inner pain just by living through it. And in biographies, the protagonist may go through many highs and lows of achievement and failure as we follow her life from beginning to end.

"But successful Hollywood movies follow a stricter formula (and if you consider 'formula' a dirty word, screenwriting may not be your most fulfilling path as a writer). Movie heroes also pursue acceptance, or revenge, and may also want to resolve relationships or inner conflicts. But if these goals don't grow out of clearly defined outer motivations, the movies simply won't get produced, or won't successfully reach a mass audience.

"In *Titanic*, Rose longs for passion and adventure; in *Shrek*, the hero would love to be accepted and find true love; and the heroes of *Star Wars*, *Working Girl*, and *Stand by Me* all need to accept themselves and stand up for who they truly are. But all of these invisible inner motivations would be static and uninvolving if these protagonists' visible goals were not to get to America with Jack, capture the princess in order to get his land back, or stop the Empire, set up the takeover, or find the dead body.

"Movies can even tell life stories, but if the subject's life is not defined by a singular visible desire—winning Jenny's love in *Forrest Gump*, for example—the film will likely be a disappointment at the box office.

"So where does all this leave you if you want to write an adaptation?

"Rich Krevolin has filled this book with principles and methods for effectively translating existing stories into screenplays. And to all of those I would add these ideas of my own:

"*The most successful adaptations originate as stories that already have clearly defined story concepts.*

"At the time I'm writing this, the top ten adaptations of all time at the box office (not including sequels) are *Jurassic Park, Forrest Gump, Harry Potter and the Sorcerer's Stone, Shrek, How the Grinch Stole Christmas, Jaws, Batman, Lord of the Rings, Mrs. Doubtfire,* and *The Exorcist.* In every single one of these stories, the hero's visible goal is clearly defined, the logline is easy to express, and we know immediately exactly what represents success for the hero: stopping the dinosaurs; winning Jenny's love; capturing the Sorcerer's Stone; retrieving (and winning the love of) the princess; stopping Christmas in Whoville; stopping the shark; stopping the Joker; getting the ring to the volcano; getting to be with his kids; and exorcising the devil from the girl.

"If you're tackling a novel that follows a long expanse of time and multiple heroes, see if you can extract the central character and a single goal from all that you have to choose from. The more focused and finite your story concept, the more commercial your screenplay will be.

"*Avoid biographies that follow heroes through a series of big events or desires.*

"Life stories may be compelling on A&E, but as films they almost always fail at the box office, or struggle to break even. *Chaplin, The Babe, Cobb,* and *Hoffa* may be about unique, larger-than-life figures, but the movies give us nothing specific to root for, and lost a ton of money.

"There are two ways to overcome this dilemma: select subjects whose lives are devoted to a single, visible outcome (freedom for India in *Gandhi;* freedom for Scotland in *Braveheart*); or pick a single incident from the life of your subject and make that the outer motivation of your movie. The written biography of John Nash reveals an abundance of events and conflicts throughout his life, but the movie focuses specifically on his and his wife's battle against schizophrenia within a much shorter period of time. And *Erin Brockovich* is the story of a woman who wants to win a lawsuit against PG&E [Pacific Gas and Electric]—none of the rest of her life is included.

"Your allegiance must be to the movie, not the source material.

"Because the goal of all story is to elicit emotion, it's easy to assume that because reading something is captivating, the screenplay of it will be as well. But novels and plays and newspaper articles operate under different rules and parameters. Florid passages of prose, deep, meaningful thoughts, or long monologues that sound good on the stage must be eliminated from your screenplay.

"Pleasing the author or the people that loved the original novel is also not your concern. Your job is to get a Hollywood executive excited about your movie, even if it means changing, or omitting altogether, your favorite parts of the book.

"It's because of this principle that you should probably . . .

"Avoid adapting your own books and plays.

"I know this comes as harsh advice for many of you, since it's probably the main reason you bought this book in the first place. But it is next to impossible to maintain the ruthless objectivity necessary to change the treasured moments of your original work in order to maintain proper movie structure. And if your manuscript sits unpublished or your play unproduced in its original form, it's unlikely it will succeed in the much more competitive world of Hollywood.

"Of course, all this changes if someone's offering you money for the film rights to your work. Once your novel or play has proven itself in its original arena, you can attach yourself as screenwriter and hope that its prior success piques Hollywood's interest.

"Of course, there are exceptions to these rules. *The Shawshank Redemption, The Green Mile, The Shipping News, Driving Miss Daisy, Terms of Endearment, A River Runs Through It, Ordinary People*— none of these films has a visible outer motivation for the hero, many cover long expanses of time, and yet they were all very successful at the box office. But they were also based on very successful books or plays, were written by well-established writers or writer/directors, and/or were driven by the stars or directors who were passionate about them. And they form a tiny percentage of the films coming out of Hollywood.

"So if you're a new writer hoping to launch your career, I'd concentrate on adaptations that give you your greatest chance of success: Stories that already contain the elements that have proven to be the foundation of Hollywood's most successful movies."

Henry Jones, a script reader for Cosgrove-Meurer, screenwriter, and reader for many major screenwriting contests, offers his thoughts below.

"Everyone critiques on story, structure, dialogue, and character. And well they should; if you lack any one of those things, your script is doomed. I've thrown more than my share into the garbage as a result of their bankruptcy in these fundamentals. Too few people, however, seem concerned with the prose itself. Nothing will get the last three months of your life (you're lucky if it only took you that long) recycled into grocery bags and cheap toilet paper faster than shoddy writing.

"Hone your craft. Worry about your story on the sentence level, on the level of a single word choice. It makes a difference. Even if the agency or producer doesn't like the story, they will accept your future submissions if they like the way you write. Be clear, be concise, but be creative. Learn to write first, then worry about plot, character, structure, story, and dialogue.

"Use as few adverbs as possible. No one runs quickly, they sprint. If you don't walk, you trot or jog, if you don't jog, you run, if you don't run, you sprint. The point is that there's almost always one word that can encapsulate what you want to say without the use of passive voice. Get rid of as many 'ly's' as you can. When you feel the need to project an emotion that you don't want the reader to miss, use your skills as a wordsmith. Don't take the easy way out. Tacking an 'ly' onto the end of a word often makes it clumsy as well. Here's an example: He looks at her lovingly. It hurts me just to write it. It describes what the person is doing, yes. But only what they're doing, not what they feel. You're saying what they feel, but you have to get the reader involved. Help them see it through your character's eyes. Try something like this: Her face is as soft and sweet as grade-school love. Now it's not just what the character sees, it's what the reader sees. Don't tell the reader what to feel. Guide them, give them the information that leads them down the emotional road you want them to travel.

"Know the difference between active and passive voice. Tighten your description. Pare down your dialogue until all that is left is what absolutely needs to be said. Write often, write well, and the rest will follow."

Professor Richard Walter, screenwriting chair, UCLA Department of Film and Television, and author of *Screenwriting—The Art, Craft, and Business of Film and Television Writing* and *The Whole Picture—Strategies for Screenwriting Success in the New Hollywood*, had these thoughts.

"What does a writer owe the original material when he is adapting it into a screenplay?

"Nothing!

"The creditor is not the original work but the movie audience, and what they are owed is the best movie possible. This invariably means excising much of the original material. If you mess up, you have not destroyed the original material, but merely made one more bad movie, which is regrettable, of course, but hardly the end of civilization. Ideally, writers should not be adapting other material but writing original screenplays. The studios prefer sequels and remakes for the same reason they like adaptations. They've been 'tested' in the market.

"But this, it seems to me, represents the suffocation of the imagination. If you read a truly great book, then that is its medium. Great books make lousy movies. The great adaptations occur when the writer is not true to the original material but true, instead, to the audience."

Robin Russin is a visiting professor of screenwriting at UCLA and co-author of *Screenplay: Writing the Picture*. He is a former Rhodes scholar, with credits including *On Deadly Ground* and *Vital Signs* on ABC, *The Luneburg Variation* and *Alcatraz: The Escape* on Fox Television. Here are some of his ideas about adaptations.

"Having adapted one novel and three true-life stories, what I look for are the story elements that reflect and contribute to the central theme I've decided best suits the material. Is it a story about discovery? About revenge? About star-crossed love? Anything that doesn't somehow relate to this central theme, either by reinforcing it or creating a dramatic contrast with it, has to go. Real life, and even many novels, can be sloppy. There are digressions, interesting events, characters, and locations that simply do not add anything to the core story, so they have to be cut or somehow combined with those that do. This can be painful, especially when dealing with a beloved novel or fascinating person. But a screenplay must be tight and focused; there simply isn't room for everything.

"Similarly, in certain cases I may *improve* on the original, where actions, motivations, or climaxes seem fuzzy or disconnected from the central action or theme. This is what Steve Zaillian and the other screenwriters who adapted *Hannibal* by Thomas Harris did. Harris's ending, where Clarice Starling essentially is transformed into a female Hannibal Lecter in order to be his mate, did violence to her core nature and to the theme of persistent honor in the face of the temptation of evil. So they kept her strong and honorable, fighting Lecter to the end, which worked much better—because that was the quality that made her so attractive to Lecter in the first place. The novel's ending felt dishonest because once Lecter had "converted" Clarice, she ceased to be the woman who kept the world interesting for him.

"In short, adaptation is not transcription but interpretation, and the central concern for the screenwriter has to be, *What will make it a better film?*"

Simon Rose is a multitalented writer whose credits include *The Alchemist*, *The Flying Scotsman*, and *Underdog*. He also wrote *Running Time*, the world's first interactive movie, in conjunction with Simon Beaufoy, writer of *The Full Monty*. His books include *Collins's*

Gem Classic Film Guide, The Classic Film Guide, and *The Essential Film Guide.* Here are his comments:

"You could argue that all writing is adaptation, in that you are having to transfer an idea from brain to paper or in that the idea for the script might itself have been suggested by something you read in a newspaper or a story you heard that gives you the idea of wondering 'what if???' But I guess you're really talking about taking someone else's idea, be it a computer game, novel, play, short story, or even Christmas card (yes, *It's a Wonderful Life* started out as a Christmas card, so I'm not completely mad).

"My first-ever script was an adaptation of a modern true-life story. This was the tale that made me get off my butt and stop talking about wanting to write screenplays, a tale so exciting that even this sport-hater had to write it. In the mid to late nineties a destitute Scotsman, Graeme Obree, whose hobby was bicycle racing, designed a revolutionary bike and built it out of bits of scrap metal and cannibalized parts of a washing machine, becoming world champion. He even had the good sense to organize this feat in three acts, with the second act bringing the world cycling authorities down on his head to try to get him out of the sport altogether, banning his bike, and the third act his designing ANOTHER revolutionary bike out of bits of scrap metal and becoming world champion YET AGAIN.

"I spent some time talking to him and researching the story. I was lucky that some of his feats had been captured in a documentary and got something of the essence of the man talking to those who had been in close contact with him. I was very careful to tell him that he might not recognize himself on screen and to insist that he not be given script approval.

"Although I needed to keep to reality when it came to his wife and child, I had to fictionalize those around him—friends, managers, et cetera—because so many people had come into Graeme's life and then gone away again. Graeme was reluctant for me to meet his wife, and I was gratified to discover that when I DID finally meet her, she and Graeme had exactly the sort of bantering, 'what's he doing now?' sort of relationship that I had imagined.

"With a story that revolves around certain sporting facts, I had to use these as the framework around which to hang the rest of the story, to determine what drove him and to ensure that the script adhered to the usual principles of getting an audience to root for someone, placing growing obstacles in his way which he managed to surmount and so on.

"It's a nice script. Simon Beaufoy, of *The Full Monty* fame, says it's one of the best he's ever read. But the Scottish producer who has it is always that little bit short of complete financing, so it may never see the light of day. Peter Chelsom, director of *Serendipity*, was going to direct it at one time, but things didn't work out.

"One of the most important lessons I'd pass on to any writer, though, is a very practical one. Because Graeme is alive, I had to get him to assign me the rights to his life. I had to reassign these to the producer at the same time as he optioned the script. And although, at a certain date, the script will revert to me, the producer has, naturally, had to get Graeme to extend HIS rights. So even if I get my script back, it will be useless, as the producer is now the one dealing with Graeme. That never occurred to me at the time but would certainly put me off doing a modern true-life story again.

"My second script, coincidentally, was also a true-life story. It was about a British sergeant in the RAF who, although he didn't know it, had multiple sclerosis. He was voted *head man* by a growing number of RAF and later army prisoners in POW camps, who ran a spy network from within Germany, to the extent of having one prisoner who LIVED at large in Germany working on establishing an escape route. At the end of the war, he had to keep order among 12,000 starving men forced by the Germans to march on the roads in deteriorating conditions toward the end of the Third Reich. Bombed by our side by mistake, with thirty or more dead, this guy persuaded the Germans to let him ride through their lines on a bike (another bike!) to tell the Allies where they were. Then, instead of going home to see the wife he hadn't seen in four years, he went back through the lines again to bring his men out. This was commissioned and the script editor loved the second draft. Unfortunately, the producer did not. He had his vision of what the film should be about and I just couldn't believe in what he was saying. So it's languishing in a drawer.

"The problems with that were pulling out the inherently dramatic moments from a period in a man's life considered, by all those I talked to who knew him, as the greatest person they'd ever known. It was VERY hard to get a handle on him, as no one seemed able to describe his personality well, the only word in common from everyone being 'stubborn.' Much of the spy stuff had to go, as it wasn't inherently dramatic, and events had to be telescoped so that there weren't innumerable bits of text on screen telling us where and when we were. In fact, I worked hard to avoid this.

"My third script was an adaptation of a cult fantasy novel about a couple of layabouts who spend most of their time in a pub who are torn between saving the world from an alien invasion and the all-important forthcoming darts championship. It was a quirky book, and I believe I wrote a similarly quirky script. To date, I have found NO ONE who appreciates the script's sense of humor.

"I'm sure that the usual things said about adaptation are right and sensible. Don't feel you have to stick too close to a story, or you may as well listen to a talking book or watch a documentary. Films have to have a beginning, middle, and an end, they have to have a dramatic shape to them that isn't necessarily there in a book or somebody's life. The worry always, and I have been guilty of this, is that you fall in love with source material and find it hard to be brutal about what you leave out. But you can't include everything, no matter how fantastic a scene is or how extraordinary an event in somebody's life. To my mind, this is amply demonstrated by *Harry Potter,* where they have tried so hard to be faithful to the author's vision that children I took are grumbling because it doesn't look the way they imagined it and they have crammed so much of the book in that it is dramatically dull at times, despite being written by one of the greatest of current screenwriters."

Sharon Y. Cobb has written *On Hostile Ground* (TBS), *Return of the Sweet Birds* (Fox, 2000), and *A Flight of Fancy* (2002). Here is what she had to say:

"I've adapted several true-life stories for the screen. Because producers have approached me to write these projects, they haven't been something I've chosen randomly. Perhaps the easiest to adapt was a movie based on the true story of Harry Bridges, the Australian who came to America for a better life and became the leader of the bloodiest labor strike in U.S. history. Although Bridges led an extraordinary life and was a fascinating man, the one event which stood out as the most dramatic was the longshoremen's strike of 1934 and the savage battle with San Francisco police officers and scabs that would become known as Bloody Thursday.

"When I first signed on to the project I was certain that the second act would focus on the few weeks leading up to Bloody Thursday and that act three would be the battle with police which culminated in the deaths of two strikers, but what I wasn't clear on was how to begin the first act. Should I start with Harry Bridges at age twenty-one sailing into the port of San Francisco, or begin with Bridges at thirty-two just before the strike began? And how would I show moments from his boyhood in Melbourne that created the passion in him to defend the rights of the poor as well as empower others to stand up for themselves?

"I wasn't keen on flashbacks, so I finally decided to begin with fifteen-year-old Harry collecting rent for his father from poverty-stricken tenants and how Harry's compassion shaped his future. Then I had to achieve a seamless time jump to age seventeen, when he talked his father into allowing him to become a merchant seaman and therefore witness and experience mistreatment of sailors and waterside workers. The next time jump was when he was twenty-one and arriving in the port of San Francisco. I chose to tie these jumps together with the thematic images of water, which I think worked quite well.

"One of the interesting things I learned while writing the Harry Bridges script, *Bloody Thursday,* is that sometimes it's difficult to know the real truth of events in someone's life. Newspaper accounts told one story, eyewitnesses another, and public records, like police reports, quite a different tale. Each party had its own agenda and reasons to record history as it did. The job of the writer is to balance those ulterior motives and come up with a dramatic point of view that tells the story you see in your head and hope to see on the screen. This is a project that was intended to be a cable movie, but a star is currently reading the script and it will certainly become a feature if this actor is interested.

"Another true story that I am currently working on is based on the life of Sarah Bernhardt. Now that's a bear of a story to wrestle to the ground. Bernhardt was a legend and lived a chaotic, exciting life. Trying to capture the essence of her story in a two-hour film has been problematic. Should I focus on one specific time period, or create the story around several times in her life?

"The most dramatic events in her long life were sprinkled throughout the years, so should I ignore the actual dates of the events and write them as if they happened within a relatively few years? Because the producers and I have met with a well-known, amazingly talented actress who is interested in the role of Bernhardt, I am shaping the story to focus on the years that she could play, so we won't be including Bernhardt's younger years. That narrowed down the narrative somewhat. Because Mademoiselle Bernhardt, even in her more mature years, led a full life, there was an abundance of story elements to include in the structure. But that created an issue of how to make the events less episodic and more cohesive. So I asked myself, what was Bernhardt's goal in her life? What themes surfaced repeatedly?

"After extensive research I discovered that the woman wanted to be immortal, and she achieved this through her acting career in the theater and silent films. I based the three-act structure around her search for immortality and her rise to fame as the world's first superstar. Then I took important relationships to her and set them all around a world tour. I took the most dramatic things that happened during numerous tours and wove them into one specific tour. Essentially, the story now represents the essence of Bernhardt's life and is organized into a narrative that accommodates a strong forward movement.

"Another true story I am currently writing started with a director coming to me with an idea based on the life of the only non-Japanese internee of the Japanese-American relocation camps of the early forties. My concern was that the young man was only seventeen when he went into the camps and there was no leading role for a star. Faces get movies made, so I suggested that we create a character that could be played by a prominent actor. So the story now revolves around the relationship of the real-life internee who followed his Japanese friends into the camps, a Caucasian teacher (the star's role), and a young Japanese woman the teacher falls in love with. The teacher is a composite inspired by several real-life adult education instructors at the camps. Once I created the characters, the story almost wrote itself.

"There was a riot in the camp where the story takes place, so I knew that would be the climax of the story and I worked backward from there. A major production company has signed on to produce, and we're pitching it to cable networks currently. I believe that an adaptation based on a true-life story must include one essential item: a compelling person who has accomplished an extraordinary thing or things. And it's certainly simpler to shape a story around a specific incident if that's the truth of the person's story. For some reason I have been drawn to period stories recently and enjoy creating the unique world of various eras. I find writing about characters who lived a more sane existence gratifying. Life without e-mail, cell phones, and Starbucks appeals to me immensely, so I enjoy experiencing a simpler time through these historical characters."

Frederick Levy is a producer/manager at "A" Management. His credits include *The Four Feathers*, *Impostor*, and *Reindeer Games*, and he is the author of *Hollywood 101: The Film Industry* and *The Hollywood Way*. This is what Fred had to say:

"I hate when people tell me that the movie wasn't the same as the book. They're two different entities. To me, it's like comparing apples and oranges. A novel is often 400 to 500 pages. A screenplay is 120 pages. How could you even expect them to be the same? They're two different mediums, each with its own rules and conventions. Books are often internal. Movies are extremely visual and dialogue-based.

"When I work on an adaptation, I look for a screenwriter who can capture the essence of the book in his/her screenplay. What did I love most about the book? How can we translate that to the screen? What will work on the screen? What will not work? Sometimes this is difficult to do. Sometimes leaving out something you love because it won't translate to the screen is harder to do than choosing what to include.

"Also, what new ideas can this writer fuse with the original material to create this new piece of work? Can the writer bring a new perspective to the story, helping us see it in a way we haven't seen it before? Most importantly, at the end of the day, can we do justice to our source material without compromising its integrity?

"Here's another problem. Are you judging an adaptation by comparing screenplay to novel, or are you comparing the novel to the final film? Since a movie is written three times (on the page, in production, in the cutting room), making the latter comparison may not be a fair assessment."

Bibliography

Akutagawa, Ryunosuke. *Rashomon and Other Stories*. Translated by Takashi Kojima. New York: Liveright Publishers, 1952.

Darabont, Frank. *The Shawshank Redemption*, with an introduction by Stephen King. The Newmarket Shooting Script Series. New York: Newmarket Press, 1996.

Homer. *The Odyssey*. Translated by John Fitzgerald. New York: Random House, 1987.

King, Stephen. *Rita Hayworth and the Shawshank Redemption*, in *Different Seasons*. New York: Viking Press, 1982.

Kurosawa, Akira, and Shinobu Hashimoto. *Rashomon* [screenplay]. New York: Grove Press, 1969.

Mamet, David. *Glengarry Glen Ross*, in *Best American Plays, Ninth Series, 1983–1992*. Edited by Clive Barnes. New York: Crown Publishers, 1993.

McKellen, Ian, and Richard Loncraine. *William Shakespeare's Richard III*. New York: Overlook Press, 1996.

Naylor, Phyllis Reynolds. *Shiloh*. New York: Atheneum Books, 1991.

Rowling, J. K. *Harry Potter and the Sorcerer's Stone*. New York: Scholastic Press, 1998.

Vogler, Christopher. *The Writer's Journey*. Studio City, Calif.: Michael Wiese Productions, 1992.

Weems, Mason Locke, and P. Horry. *The Life of General Francis Marion*, 1809. Reprint, with new introduction, Winston-Salem, N.C.: John F. Blair Publishers, 2000.

Filmography

Apocalypse Now. Directed by Francis Ford Coppola; written by Michael Herr, John Milius, and Francis Ford Coppola. United Artists, 1979.

Batman. Directed by Tim Burton; written by Sam Hamm and Warren Skaaren. Warner Brothers, 1989.

Blade Runner. Directed by Ridley Scott; written by Hampton Fancher and David Peoples. Warner Brothers, 1982.

Braveheart. Directed by Mel Gibson; written by Randall Wallace. Twentieth Century Fox, 1995.

Citizen Kane. Directed by Orson Welles; written by Orson Welles and Herman Mankiewicz. RKO Radio Pictures, 1941.

Driving Miss Daisy. Directed by Bruce Beresford; written by Alfred Uhry. Warner Brothers, 1989.

The English Patient. Directed by Anthony Minghella; written by Anthony Minghella. Miramax, 1996.

Erin Brockovich. Directed by Steven Soderbergh; written by Susannah Grant. Columbia TriStar, 2000.

Evita. Directed by Alan Parker; written by Alan Parker. Hollywood Pictures, 1996.

The Exorcist. Directed by William Friedkin; written by William Peter Blatty. Warner Brothers, 1973.

Firestarter. Directed by Mark L. Lester; written by Stanley Mann III. Universal Pictures, 1984.

Forrest Gump. Directed by Robert Zemeckis; written by Eric Roth. Paramount, 1994.

Friday the 13th. Directed by Sean S. Cunningham; written by Victor Miller. Paramount, 1980.

Glengarry Glen Ross. Directed by James Foley; written by David Mamet. New Line Cinema, 1992.

Glory. Directed by Edward Zwick; written by Kevin Jarre. Tri-Star, 1989.

The Godfather. Directed by Francis Ford Coppola; written by Francis Ford Coppola and Mario Puzo. Paramount, 1972.

The Godfather Part II. Directed by Francis Ford Coppola; written by Francis Ford Coppola and Mario Puzo. Paramount, 1974.

The Graduate. Directed by Mike Nichols; written by Calder Willingham and Buck Henry. Embassy Pictures, 1967.

The Green Mile. Directed by Frank Darabont; written by Frank Darabont. Warner Brothers, 1999.

Harry Potter and the Sorcerer's Stone. Directed by Chris Columbus; written by Steven Kloves. Warner Brothers, 2001.

How the Grinch Stole Christmas. Directed by Ron Howard; written by Jeffrey Price. Imagine Entertainment, 2000.

In the Heat of the Night. Directed by Norman Jewison; written by Stirling Silliphant. United Artists, 1967.

Jaws. Directed by Steven Spielberg; written by Peter Benchley, Carl Gottlieb, and Howard Sackler. Universal Pictures, 1975.

The Jazz Singer. Directed by Alan Crosland; written by Alfred Cohn and Jack Jarmuth. Warner Brothers, 1927.

Jurassic Park. Directed by Steven Spielberg; written by David Koepp, Michael Crichton, and Malia Scotch Marmo. Universal Pictures, 1993.

The Lion King. Directed by Roger Allers and Robert Minkoff; written by Irene Macchi. Disney, 1994.

Lord of the Rings: The Fellowship of the Ring. Directed by Peter Jackson; written by Frances Walsh. New Line Cinema, 2001.

The Lost World: Jurassic Park. Directed by Steven Spielberg; written by David Koepp. Universal Pictures, 1997.

Madison. Directed by William Bindley; written by Scott and William Bindley. Premiere Entertainment, 2002.

Monty Python's Life of Brian. Directed by Terry Jones; written by John Cleese. Orion Pictures, 1979.

Mrs. Doubtfire. Directed by Chris Columbus; written by Randi Mayem Singer and Leslie Dixon. Twentieth Century Fox, 1993.

Notting Hill. Directed by Roger Mitchell; written by Richard Curtis. Polygram Filmed Entertainment, 1999.

O Brother, Where Art Thou? Directed by Joel Coen; written by Ethan and Joel Coen. Buena Vista Pictures, 2000.

On the Waterfront. Directed by Elia Kazan; written by Budd Schulberg. Columbia, 1954.

Ordinary People. Directed by Robert Redford; written by Alvin Sargent. Paramount, 1980.

The Outrage. Directed by Martin Ritt; written by Michael Kanin, based upon a screenplay by Akira Kurosawa. MGM, 1964.

The Patriot. Directed by Roland Emmerich; written by Robert Rodat. Columbia, 2000.

Phenomenon. Directed by Jon Turtletaub; written by Gerald DiPego. Touchstone, 1996.

The Player. Directed by Robert Altman; written by Michael Tolkin. Fine Line, 1992.

Pretty Woman. Directed by Garry Marshall; written by J. F. Lawton. Touchstone, 1990.

The Producers. Directed by Mel Brooks; written by Mel Brooks. Avco Embassy Pictures, 1967.

Psycho. Directed by Alfred Hitchcock; written by Joseph Stefano. Paramount, 1960.

Quiz Show. Directed by Robert Redford; written by Paul Attanasio. Hollywood Pictures, 1994.

Raging Bull. Directed by Martin Scorsese; written by Paul Schrader and Mardik Martin. United Artists, 1980.

Rashomon. Directed by Akira Kurosawa; written by Shinobu Hashimoto. RKO, 1950.

Richard III. Directed by Richard Loncraine; written by Richard Loncraine and Ian McKellen. MGM, 1995.

A River Runs Through It. Directed by Robert Redford; written by Richard Friedenberg. Columbia, 1992.

The Seventh Seal. Directed by Ingmar Bergman; written by Ingmar Bergman. Svensk, 1957.

The Shawshank Redemption. Directed by Frank Darabont; written by Frank Darabont. Columbia, 1994.

Shiloh. Directed by Dale Rosenbloom; written by Dale Rosenbloom. Legacy Releasing, 1997.

Shrek. Directed by Andrew Adamson and Vicky Jenson; written by Ted Elliott and Terry Rossio. Dreamworks SKG, 2001.

Sleepless in Seattle. Directed by Nora Ephron; written by Nora Ephron, David S. Ward, and Jeff Arch. Columbia, 1993.

Snow White, a Tale of Terror. Directed by Michael Cohn; written by Thomas E. Szollosi and Deborah Serra. Interscope, 1997.

Splash. Directed by Ron Howard; written by Lowell Ganz, Babaloo Mandel, and Bruce Jay Friedman. Touchstone, 1984.

Stand by Me. Directed by Rob Reiner; written by Raynold Gideon and Bruce A. Evans. Columbia, 1986.

Star Trek. Directed by Robert Wise; written by Harold Livingston and Gene Roddenberry. Paramount, 1979.

Star Wars. Directed by George Lucas; written by George Lucas. Twentieth Century Fox, 1977.

Terms of Endearment. Directed by James L. Brooks; written by James L. Brooks. Paramount, 1983.

Titanic. Directed by James Cameron; written by James Cameron. Twentieth Century Fox, 1997.

To Kill a Mockingbird. Directed by Robert Mulligan; written by Horton Foote. Universal Pictures, 1962.

Toy Story. Directed by John Lasseter; written by John Lasseter, Andrew Stanton, Peter Ducter, and Joe Ranft. Disney, 1995.

2001: A Space Odyssey. Directed by Stanley Kubrick; written by Stanley Kubrick and Arthur C. Clarke. MGM, 1968.

Wayne's World. Directed by Penelope Spheeris; written by Mike Myers, Bonnie Turner, and Terry Turner. Paramount, 1992.

When Harry Met Sally. Directed by Rob Reiner; written by Nora Ephron. Columbia, 1989.

The Wizard of Oz. Directed by Victor Fleming and King Vidor; written by Noel Langley, Florence Ryerson, and Edgar Allan Woolf. MGM, 1939.

Working Girl. Directed by Mike Nichols; written by Kevin Wade. Twentieth Century Fox, 1988.

X-Men. Directed by Bryan Singer; written by Tom DeSanto and Bryan Singer. Twentieth Century Fox, 2000.

About the Author

Richard Krevolin is an author, playwright, screenwriter, and professor. A graduate of Yale University, Richard went on to earn a master's degree in screenwriting at UCLA's School of Theater, Film and Television and a master's degree in playwriting and fiction from USC. He is an adjunct professor of screenwriting at USC in the cinema/TV department and also teaches at the UCLA film and TV department. He is the author of the books *Screenwriting from the Soul* and *Pilot Your Life,* which was written with Pilot Pen CEO Ronald Shaw.

Richard has several screenplays under option and in development. He was a finalist for the $500,000 Kingman Screenwriting Award, the Chesterfield Contest, the Klasky-Csupo Screenwriting Contest, and the Nicholl Fellowship Screenwriting Award. He won the USC One-Act Play Festival for his comedy *Love Is Like Velcro.* His play *Trotsky's Garden* was a finalist for the Eugene O'Neill National Playwrights' Conference. His one-man show *Yahrzeit,* a finalist in the HBO New Writer's Project, was a huge hit at the Santa Monica Playhouse, running for five sold-out months; under a new name, *Boychik,* it opened Off-Broadway at Theater Four in New York City in 1997 and regularly is performed.

He received Valley Theatre League nominations for best director and best play for his one-man musical *Rebbe Soul-O.* His play *King Levine* opened in February 1999 at the Odyssey Theater under the direction of Joseph Bologna and, after receiving rave reviews, transferred to the Tiffany. It was also nominated for an Ovation Award as Best Adaptation. In 2001, Richard had two one-person plays open in Los Angeles, *The Lemony Fresh Scent of Diva Monsoon* (starring Ruth DeSosa) at the Rose Alley and *Seltzer Man* (starring David Proval of *The Sopranos*) at the Tiffany. His plays have been performed by Ed Asner, Allen Arbus, Jean Smart, Mackenzie Phillips, and Richard Kline.

Besides his talents as a writer, Richard has been motivating and inspiring students through his teaching at USC since 1988; in addition, he has also taught at UCLA, Pepperdine University, the University of Redlands, Ithaca College, and Los Angeles Community College. He is the main sponsor for the Screenwriting from the Soul Annual Script Competition, which is dedicated to finding the most heartwarming script in America. In addition, he is an affiliated artist with the Center for Jewish Culture and Creativity and conducts writers' workshops and seminars throughout the world, including regular seminars for PlanetaryVoices.com in Lake Tahoe. His web site is www.ProfK.com, and he can be reached at Krevolin@usc.edu or at rkrevolin@yahoo.com.